F·R·O·M
BONDAGE
TO
BONDING

A WORKING GUIDE TO RECOVERY FROM CODEPENDENCY AND OTHER INJURIES OF THE HEART

NANCY GROOM

NAVPRESS ◐
A MINISTRY OF THE NAVIGATORS
P.O.BOX 35001, COLORADO SPRINGS, COLORADO 80935

The Navigators is an international Christian organization. Jesus Christ gave His followers the Great Commission to go and make disciples (Matthew 28:19). The aim of The Navigators is to help fulfill that commission by multiplying laborers for Christ in every nation.

NavPress is the publishing ministry of The Navigators. NavPress publications are tools to help Christians grow. Although publications alone cannot make disciples or change lives, they can help believers learn biblical discipleship, and apply what they learn to their lives and ministries.

Printed in the United States of America

CONTENTS

To Mary, Peg, and Thom—
who grew up with me in my home
and who still live in my heart.

PREFACE

Philosophy and Purpose of This Guide

The workshop experience outlined in this book is intended to help concerned people deal with the difficulties they face in their relationships with others. The particular problem named in this guide is *codependency,* but there are also many other kinds of compulsions that control people's lives and disrupt or destroy their relationships. Substance addictions, workaholism, eating disorders, sexual abuse and addictions, shopping or gambling compulsions, physical or emotional abuse—these are just some of the problems that control men and women, as well as those who live with them. This working guide offers hope for lives damaged not only by codependency, but also by these other kinds of dysfunctions.

Codependency and other life-controlling problems never operate in a vacuum. They are essentially *communal* rather than *individual,* sabotaging interpersonal freedom and authenticity in the communities where we live—in our families, in our churches, in our neighborhoods. Because our codependency and compulsions have been developed and lived out in community, it seems fitting to turn to community (the small group) to heal the wounds we have both experienced and inflicted. In the small-group context we can learn to discard our codependent, compulsive strategies and instead embrace honest sharing, open-eyed forgiveness, and mutual encouragement. We can become the mutually interdependent members of Christ's Body we were meant to be.

Jesus Christ spent a lot of time in "small-group ministry" with His disciples and close friends, preparing them for the larger (and later) work of bringing His Kingdom to a desperately needy world. It is appropriate that we follow His example.

This working guide for Christ-centered recovery from codependency and other life-controlling problems offers practical, step-by-step guidelines for small groups of believers who wish to address the issues that keep them trapped in destructive ways of conducting relationships. Included in this workbook are specific individual and group exercises that will help participants understand their own wrong styles of relating to God, self, and others.

The group process provides a setting in which people can experience repentance, forgiveness, and mutual love in their journey into healing. The goal of this guided group experience is not just that group members become less compulsive or less codependent, but that they become more Christlike and more God-dependent. Emphasis is placed on developing a personal, vibrant relationship with God that overflows in compassionate movement toward others, beginning with your fellow participants in these small groups.

What This Guide Has to Offer

To accomplish the goal of healing and spiritual growth, this workbook is designed with activities to be worked through individually, in small groups, or in the larger healing community. Each session will include the following:

- Explanation of two or three concepts related to understanding and recovering from codependency and other life-controlling problems.

- Exercises for individual reflection and self-evaluation.

- Opportunities for personal disclosure in a group setting.

- Study of Scripture relevant to each session's theme.

- Vehicles for mutual commitment, encouragement, and affirmation.

- Practice in group and individual prayer.

- Opportunities for personal assessment regarding codependency and spiritual growth.

- Treatment of the steps in AA's Twelve-Step recovery process, where applicable.

- Weekly "homework"—not study, but a chance to practice change outside the group setting.

- Suggested meditation theme and Bible passages for personal study.

To facilitate healing, each session will focus on one theme related to codependency and other life-controlling problems. To facilitate spiritual growth, each session will also center on one attribute of God. The assumption is that a distorted idea of what God is really like lies at the root of many of our struggles, even for those of us well-trained in church doctrine and practice. This guide follows the concepts (though not the outline) of the book *From Bondage to Bonding* by Nancy Groom.

How to Use This Guide

To make it easy to use, this guide provides a thorough map for working through the material. Details like how long to spend on each exercise, how many people per group, and the order of sessions are all suggested so that a group leader is not obliged to design the meeting structure if he or she prefers not to.

However, nothing about the structure is sacred. Exercises can be omitted; sessions can be divided in two; a facilitator might even decide to select six or eight sessions scattered through the guide that will best meet the needs of his or her unique group. For instance, one might want to focus on losses, or rebonding, or on those sessions that deal with the Twelve Steps explicitly. Likewise, the twenty-four-week program divides easily into four six-week modules or two twelve-week modules. And if a group has more than ninety minutes per session or wants to give more or less attention to a particular exercise, the suggested time allotments are negotiable.

Each session will focus on a particular topic related to codependency or compulsion. This working guide contains not only the material to read and questions to discuss, but also space for writing individual exercises and printed Bible passages for easy reference. Each participant should bring his or her own copy of the guide to each meeting. Bibles may be helpful at times, but they are optional. Session 1 contains much more detailed information about how the sessions are designed.

Suggestions for Leaders

Two types of leadership functions will help the program run smoothly: the *large group facilitator* (who will oversee the entire group) and the *family group leaders* (one leader for every six or eight participants). If the entire group contains fewer than ten people, it makes sense to combine the facilitator and small-group leader functions. Because the roles of each type of leader are clear, you can use this guide equally well in a large Sunday school class, a home group, or any other sort of recovery group. (You can even use it on your own, but the group adds a valuable dimension.)

The facilitator will be responsible for opening and closing each weekly meeting on time for the combined group. He or she will read the introduction and announce the warm-up activity before participants move into their individual or family group exercises. The facilitator will also reconvene the group about ten minutes before the end of each session to read the "Word of Hope" section, invite questions about the "During the Week" homework, and speak the words of benediction.

In addition, for the first few sessions (or as long as seems necessary), the facilitator will announce when it is time for participants in the smaller family groups to move from one activity to the next. Increasingly, however, each family group should be able to take responsibility for its own time frame, remaining flexible enough to be sensitive to the needs of all family group members.

If the group is large, chairs might be initially in rows. People will have to move chairs when they form temporary family groups. However, once the family groups are permanent, that chair moving and arranging won't be necessary if the chairs are arranged in small circles at the beginning of the meeting. The introduction and warm-up should work with people already sitting in family groups.

The facilitator may assign family group leaders, or each family group can choose its own leader—temporarily in the beginning, and then permanently when groups are fixed in session 3. A third option is for members to take turns leading their groups.

Because the family group leader sets the tone for the family group, it would be a good idea to select leaders who have some experience dealing personally with issues such as addiction, denial, dysfunctional relationships, and anger toward self, others, and God. If the leader sets an example of honesty about his or her own wounds and sin, the rest of the group will find it much easier to be honest. The leader also must be aware of deeper issues the members are struggling with, and be prepared to direct them toward professional counseling when necessary.

The family group leader's first task is to read through each session in this guide before the meeting so he or she will know what to expect. It may also be helpful to read a session ahead to prepare for what's coming up. During the meeting, he or she will move the group through the activities, remaining sensitive to all group members. When time is limited, it's helpful for someone to take the job of saying, "I think we've exhausted that subject. Let's move on," or "I think we're on a tangent here. Let's go back to the main question: 'Why do you suppose . . . ?'" If a leader sees a particular discussion of a question as especially fruitful, he or she might suggest that the group take extra time on that one and skip the next one.

The family group leader is responsible to encourage (but not force) participation from all group members, and to discourage whatever hinders the group process, such as advice-giving, judgmentalism, lengthy monologues, breaching confidentiality, and so on. He or she must be prayerfully sensitive to the leading of the Holy Spirit in dealing with people, encouraging them toward spiritual growth through homework, personal Bible reading, and family group prayer support.

For further help in understanding group dynamics and working out problems within the group, take advantage of such resources as Neal McBride's book, *How to Lead Small Groups*, published by NavPress.

Bon Voyage

Those who have participated in writing this guide pray that you will find hope and healing for damaged and damaging relationships through involvement in Christ-centered small groups. As you move from codependency and compulsion to mutual freedom and responsible authenticity, we pray that God the Father's grace may surround your journey and lead you faithfully home.

ACKNOWLEDGMENTS

This working guide, intended to foster the Holy Spirit's work of healing damaged lives through the group process, owes much to the "group" who surrounded and nurtured me during its creation:

To my much-loved husband, Bill, for his courage to face himself, his readiness to obey the Father, and his deep abiding love for me.

To our dear son, Christopher, for his unrelenting honesty, his determined quest for what is true, and his ability to make me laugh with sheer pleasure.

To the faithful friends in my support group, for their willingness to confront and to comfort me in delicate balance.

And to my wonderful editor, Karen Hinckley, for her giftedness and her integrity—not letting me run from my struggle nor running from her own, but grappling with me to discern the Father's will for this book.

For all these and for the countless other who have honored me by sharing their hearts and their stories, I proclaim again with gladness: Thanks be to God!

PART ONE

LONGINGS AND LOSSES

WHAT IS CODEPENDENCY?

LARGE GROUP

Facilitator: Beginning with yourself and proceeding around the room, let group members take turns reading aloud paragraphs of this introductory section. Read down to the heading "Warm-up."
(10 minutes)

Welcome to this gathering! You're meeting with others who want to learn about codependency. Perhaps you suspect you may be codependent, or possibly you're wondering if the title fits someone else you know. In these first few sessions, we'll explore what codependency is and where it comes from. After that, we'll look at how a person can escape the bondage of codependency and become someone who really loves well.

The others in the group are here for the same reasons: to understand, face, and find a freedom from the bondage in their lives. For the group to work, you will need to become increasingly able to trust each other with the truth about what's inside each of you. Since it's unreasonable to trust total strangers, you'll have opportunities to get to know each other as the weeks go by.

As with any group endeavor, certain assumptions and expectations will guide us in our pursuit of healing and deeper spirituality.

Participation Guidelines

REGULAR ATTENDANCE
- Healing will be enhanced if we commit to meeting regularly with this healing community.
- Attending meetings and confronting our pain are essential to the healing process.

HONEST SHARING
- Identifying our true feelings is an important goal during the healing process.
- Sharing our true feelings with fellow participants will build trust and deepen relationships.
- Telling the truth will be done in the context of genuine concern for others.

ATTENTIVE LISTENING
- Letting others speak without interrupting affirms the speaker.
- Listening with compassion does not require us to take responsibility for the speaker's feelings or actions.

• Limiting our own comments to the topic at hand and avoiding lengthy monologues will encourage mutual attention.

STRICT CONFIDENTIALITY
• Refusing to gossip or to disclose information about fellow participants is essential to promoting trust.
• When we go home, we will leave in this room everything that was said here.

MUTUAL RESPECT
• Giving advice detracts from each person's individual responsibility to make his or her own choices.
• Fixing others is not the purpose of our meeting together; only God can change a life.

WEEKLY DISCIPLINES
• Spending at least fifteen minutes a day in meditation (reading and thinking about a Scripture passage) and prayer (conversing with God) is vitally important to spiritual growth and personal healing.
• Completing the activities suggested each week in the "During the Week" sections of this workbook will greatly enhance our healing process; a "homework buddy" from the group would encourage mutual consistency.

ACCEPTANCE OF DISCOMFORT
• Change—even good change—is sometimes uncomfortable; anger and sadness are necessary aspects of our recovery.
• Healing takes time; we can learn to be patient with ourselves and others.
• Trying to be perfect is part of the problem, not part of the solution; when we make mistakes, we can offer ourselves and others the forgiveness God offers us.

During each weekly meeting of this twenty-four-week workshop there will be opportunity for two or more of the following kinds of personal or group interactions (designated by the accompanying symbols).

LARGE GROUP

These are combined healing community activities, in which the entire group will be guided by the group facilitator in opening and closing the meeting. If your group contains fewer than ten people, then your combined healing community will be the same as your family group.

FAMILY GROUP

These activities are for family group sharing, in which five to seven participants meet for discussion and self-disclosure. During session 3 of this workshop, permanent family groups will be formed to provide a predictably safe environment in which "family members" can share honestly, find encouragement, and learn to trust. To preserve that openness and trust, participation in this workshop will be open to newcomers only during the first three sessions, unless the entire group wishes to include new members after that. Each permanent family group will choose its own leader.

These are individual writing exercises, to be written either in this workbook or in your own journal. You are encouraged to purchase a notebook this week in which to complete your journaling assignments and to record what you are learning. Daily meditation discoveries and prayer requests (answers, too!) can also be included in this personal journal. Honesty is the only requirement in your journaling, not literary style or "correct" English.

Once the facilitator has introduced the "Warm-up" exercise each week, group members will follow the instructions in the workbook until the facilitator reconvenes the entire healing community to close the meeting. The time allotments for each activity are intended to help you cover each session in ninety minutes, if that is your goal. The facilitator will be the timekeeper so that others do not have to check their watches. He or she will announce when each new activity is to begin. The group and/or facilitator can, of course, change any time limits if that seems reasonable.

FAMILY GROUP

Warm-up

You'll spend much of your time in this session getting to know each other. Form groups of five to seven people (members of the same family should be in separate groups if your community is large enough). Each person in your group should do the following:

> **Facilitator:** Groups of seven will require a bit longer for the warm-up than will groups of five. If you are pressed for time, keep family groups small.
> When you call time, tell groups to begin the next exercise and continue following the written instructions.
> (10-15 minutes)

1. Tell your first name.

2. Explain why you have come to this group today. (At this point, limit your story to two minutes. Hit the highlights.)

Jenny's Story

Nothing was working anymore—not the cheerful pretense, not the subtle manipulating, not the dogged attempts at normalcy, not even the desperate prayers that God do something. "It's hopeless," Jenny's inner voice concluded. "You might as well give up."

> While you read the following story to yourself, underline phrases that describe things you can identify with. Even if the situation is quite different from yours, perhaps some feelings aren't so different. Underline emotions you've had in the past, as well as those you have now.
> (5 minutes)

Jenny sat on the edge of her bed and glanced around. Her wedding picture with Brad smiled out at her, and she wondered with a cynical laugh, "How could the promises have so betrayed us both?" The photos of the children caught in spontaneous play pierced Jenny's heart with regret and guilt now that things were so different, so awful. After twenty-six years of marriage and the raising of two daughters, Jenny felt numb and out of touch with life. Her world was closing in on her.

Brad had just returned to the store after supper. It was the same old story. He'd come home angry and half drunk again. The sale he'd planned was not going well, and his drinking would surely escalate when he came home later that night.

The fallout of Brad's anger had landed, as usual, on the family. At supper he'd complained about the food, fumed about the broken dishwasher, criticized Jenny's housework—and all the while Jenny nervously apologized. Their daughter Jodie, a high school senior, seemed immune to her father's condition and comments. After supper she'd retreated again to her bedroom without a word.

"At least Melinda is away at college, away from the responsibility she always took for her father's drinking," Jenny sighed to herself. She missed Melinda—even envied her—but she was glad her daughter could escape the craziness.

In a way, the failure of Brad's sale that particular day wasn't even the issue at all; he drank just as much when a sale went well. Jenny knew things were getting worse, but she could see no way out. With the familiar knots tightening in her stomach, she recalled the spoiled dinner parties, the missed holiday celebrations, the nights she had bundled her young girls out of bed and into the car to rescue Brad, too drunk to drive, from the downtown bar.

"What choice did I have?" she asked herself. "I couldn't let anyone see him drunk. What if the pastor had found out and Brad couldn't be a deacon anymore? What if Brad had an accident and killed someone?" At the time it seemed necessary to "save Brad from himself." But now after years of coping with his unpredictable and increasingly angry behavior, Jenny was feeling used, unappreciated, trapped, angry.

Much of Jenny's anger, of course, was unconscious. Terrified of Brad's abandonment, she refused to experience how angry she was—toward him and toward her often demanding and unappreciative daughters. No one except her closest sister knew how uncontrolled Brad's drinking had become, or how chaotic Jenny's life was because of it. She was angry, to be sure, but her anger had taken the form of martyrdom, silent withdrawal from Brad and the children, social isolation, increasing depression, and a camouflaged resentment rapidly settling into chronic bitterness—not just toward Brad but toward life in general. She felt like a puppet with its strings hanging out for anyone to pull.

"That's it," Jenny thought bitterly as the image played across her mind. "I'm everybody's marionette, yanked around day after day, dancing to whatever tune someone else wants to play. What about my tune? Why is no one meeting my needs? Will this nightmare never end?"

FAMILY GROUP

With your group of five to seven people, briefly discuss the phrases you underlined. (20 minutes)

3. In what ways do you identify with Jenny? In what ways do you see your current situation and feelings differently?

FAMILY GROUP

Remain with your family group and take turns reading this section aloud; then discuss the questions that follow.
(25 minutes)

Codependency Defined

The term *codependency* is usually related to an addiction of some kind because most codependents are or have been in a relationship with an addicted or compulsive person. In fact, even the addict is codependent, a fact that becomes obvious once the substance abuse is stopped. But in recent years codependency has been increasingly viewed as an identifiable, unhealthy compulsion in its own right. In other words, a codependent person is "addicted"—not to a destructive substance, but to a destructive pattern of relating to other people, a pattern usually learned from childhood in an abusive or non-nurturing home. Codependency holds a person hostage to other people's behaviors, moods, or opinions, and the codependent bases his or her worth and actions on someone else's life. It's a terrible bondage.

Therapists have not agreed on a clinical description of codependency, but in the next several sessions we will explore this working definition:

> Codependency is a self-focused way of life in which a person blind to his or her true self continually reacts to others, being controlled by and seeking to control their behavior, attitudes, and/or opinions. This results in spiritual sterility, loss of authenticity, and absence of intimacy.

Codependency is a matter of degree. Everyone feels controlled by people and circumstances at times; codependents feel that way most of their lives. Everyone tries to control others to some extent; codependents think they'll die if they lose control. Everyone has blind spots; but codependents live in denial about basic realities in their relationships.

Think of a relationship line that looks like this:

Debilitating _____ Healthy mutual
codependency   interdependence

Everyone falls somewhere along this line, but people who live (or used to live) in close relationship to alcoholics, drug abusers, workaholics, or other addicted persons usually occupy the codependent end of the spectrum.

There are no clear-cut indicators of just when a person steps over the line from being non-codependent to being codependent. You can't be a little bit pregnant, but you can be a little bit codependent. However, codependency is also progressive, so the longer a person pursues codependent strategies for dealing with life, the more codependent he or she becomes. Eventually those strategies become an addictive way of life, a person's primary and compulsive method for relating to God, self, and others, and we say of that person, "He (or she) is codependent."

4. Think about Jenny and discuss how her way of life might really be *self-focused*. (After all, isn't she thinking a lot about Brad, her daughters, and others?)

If self-focus and being blind to self seem contradictory now, don't worry. In later sessions you'll see how they fit together.

5. Can you identify with any of these *results* of codependency? Explain.

•I feel that I lack a vibrant, blossoming spiritual life.

•I feel like I don't know who I am.

•I'm not really close to anyone.

6. How does it feel to tell the other people in this group personal things about yourself? Are you willing to continue doing so?

FAMILY GROUP

┌─────────────────────────────────────┐
│ **Facilitator:** While the small   │
│ groups remain together, read   │
│ these instructions aloud.   │
│ (10 minutes)   │
└─────────────────────────────────────┘

Prayer Requests

Each week there will be opportunity just before the final closing for family members to request and offer prayer support to one another. These guidelines are recommended:

•Be brief and specific with your prayer request. There will be opportunity to tell your stories to the group at other times during each meeting.

•Resist the impulse to give advice or offer solutions when group members make their prayer requests.

•Each family member will volunteer to pray for one other family member during the coming week, using the form below as a reminder. Spend a few minutes right now sharing requests and offering to pray specifically for someone in your small group.

My prayer request is _____

_____

and _____ is praying for me.

I am praying for _____ and his/her prayer request is _____

LARGE GROUP

A Word of Hope

Facilitator: Gather the entire group together, and read the next four sections aloud. Get a volunteer to read Ephesians 3:20-21. (10 minutes)

Besides the healing community, two primary tools for accomplishing necessary and lasting change in our lives are the Bible (God's Word to us) and prayer (our opportunity to interact in our relationship with Him). Our journey out of codependency and into the healing of mutual love will make generous use of these two disciplines, hopefully in new and exciting ways. God's Word for us at the beginning of this journey is a word of hope from the Apostle Paul.

> **Now to him who is able to do immeasurably more than all we ask or imagine, according to his power that is at work within us, to him be glory in the church and in Christ Jesus throughout all generations, for ever and ever! (Ephesians 3:20-21)**

If the real God is at work within a person, He can do immeasurably more than we can even imagine. So if your situation seems impossible right now, have hope. God is up to something in your life, and this group can join you in asking the real God to start right now doing amazing things in and among you all.

Prayer

Spend a minute of silence together. If you know God, ask Him to start revealing and dealing with the ways in which you hurt yourself by focusing on yourself. If you've never talked to God before, you could ask Him, "God, if You're real, show me. Help me." After a moment of silence, all who wish may recite the Serenity Prayer together:

> Lord, grant me the serenity to accept the things I cannot change,
> the courage to change the things I can,
> and the wisdom to know the difference. Amen.

During the Week

Take some time alone this week to complete the assessment on the following pages. It will help you determine whether or not there are codependent issues in your life.

For more information on this week's topic, see *From Bondage to Bonding,* chapter 1. For more information regarding next week's topic, read chapter 2.

Thinking God's Thoughts

Each week a concept connected to the session's theme will be suggested for you to meditate on during the coming week whenever you have a quiet moment—perhaps during your daily meditation time or while driving or as part of your praise to God. In addition, each week six related Scripture passages will be listed and you may use them for your daily personal worship or as part of your individual healing process. A model prayer is also offered for personalizing your Bible reading. From now on, this section of the workbook will not be mentioned at the end of the meeting, but you are encouraged to take advantage of these disciplines each week.

Theme for meditation: GOD OFFERS HOPE.

Reading: Genesis 28:10-15
                      Jeremiah 29:10-14
                      Psalm 25:1-7
                      Proverbs 23:17-18
                      Luke 8:26-39
                      Romans 8:18-21

Prayer:
      Lord, thank You for this evidence in Your Word that You are a God who offers
            hope:
      Lord, thank You for this evidence in my life that I can hope in You:
      Lord, this is my creative way to show You I believe in the hope You offer:

Benediction

Hear the words of the Apostle Paul:

> **Facilitator:** Ask the group to stand while you read this section aloud.

May the grace of the Lord Jesus Christ, and the love of God, and the fellowship of the Holy Spirit be with you all. (2 Corinthians 13:14)

Personal Codependency Assessment

Put a check in front of each statement that applies to you.

Feeling Choiceless

Codependents tend to:

_____ become enmeshed in relationships with addicted, abusive, or disordered people

_____ think they don't exist unless connected to others

_____ feel compelled to do what others expect or demand

_____ hinge their happiness on others

_____ focus overmuch on the problems others cause

_____ assume responsibility for meeting others' needs to the exclusion of acknowledging their own

_____ sacrifice their values to stay connected to others

_____ value others' opinions/choices more than their own

_____ allow their moods to be determined by others' moods

_____ feel unable to quit worrying about others' problems

_____ seek love from people incapable of loving

_____ lose interest in their own lives when they love

_____ believe they can't take care of themselves

_____ feel trapped in relationships

_____ believe they can't live without certain others

_____ keep letting others hurt them

_____ think other people make them feel angry

_____ feel controlled by other people's anger

_____ disbelieve they can do anything to change things

_____ feel helpless and victimized in relationships

_____ believe about themselves what others believe

Low Self-Esteem

Codependents tend to:

_____ come from troubled or dysfunctional families

_____ deny they come from troubled or dysfunctional families

_____ feel unloved or unvalued by their parents

_____ try to prove they're good enough to be loved

_____ tolerate abuse to keep people loving them

_____ blame themselves for everything

_____ reject compliments or praise

_____ get depressed from lack of compliments or praise
_____ feel guilty spending money on themselves or having fun
_____ fear making mistakes
_____ have a hard time making decisions
_____ feel ashamed of who they are
_____ believe they don't deserve good things and happiness
_____ feel personal contempt when others fail
_____ despair of being loved and settle for being needed
_____ have a history of recurrent physical or sexual abuse
_____ suffer from stress-related medical illnesses
_____ feel good about themselves only when approved
_____ dislike and judge themselves harshly
_____ feel good about themselves only when helping others
_____ react out of a deep fear of anger, rejection, abandonment
_____ postpone or reject needed medical care as too costly
_____ wonder about their own sanity
_____ believe they have virtually no impact on others
_____ sometimes think about suicide

Control

Codependents tend to:

_____ feel inordinately responsible for other people
_____ worry about things they can't change, and try to change them anyway
_____ equate self-worth with ability to control self/others
_____ engage in hypervigilance toward self and others
_____ check on and try to control others' destructive habits
_____ rescue others from negative consequences of choices
_____ conceal, deny, or protect their dysfunctional loved one
_____ do for others what they should/could do for themselves
_____ exact promises of improved behavior from loved ones
_____ make threats without following through on them
_____ take over the dysfunctional loved one's normal duties
_____ try to rein in family finances with little success
_____ manipulate others to "do it my way" (the best/only way)
_____ dictate others' appearance/speech/behavior because it reflects on them
_____ feel safest when in charge
_____ love people they can pity and rescue
_____ feel angry when their help isn't effective
_____ anticipate other people's needs
_____ feel safest when giving
_____ feel attracted to needy people
_____ refuse to see/deal with their fear of loss of control
_____ feel bored/worthless without crisis or problem to solve
_____ try to control with helplessness, guilt, threat, advice
_____ find themselves unable to be spontaneous or have fun

Self-Sufficiency

Codependents tend to:

_____ remain in long-term committed relationships with active substance abusers without seeking outside help

_____ believe they have more power than they really do
_____ feel unable to say no, even when they know they should
_____ over-commit and over-obligate themselves
_____ keep looking for what's missing in their lives
_____ refuse to ever appear needy
_____ never ask for help
_____ consider themselves beyond the power of addiction
_____ feel alone, but won't risk self-disclosure
_____ use giving as a way to feel safe in relationships
_____ feel shame over substance abuser and withdraw from others
_____ feel smug and self-righteous toward substance abuser
_____ refuse to do what they can't do perfectly
_____ often start things they don't finish
_____ find it hard to relax even after their work is done
_____ find unpredictability distressing, even intolerable
_____ have a burning need to set things right
_____ worry about why they haven't done better
_____ remain addicted to excitement
_____ have a lot of "shoulds" and feel a lot of guilt
_____ isolate themselves from those who might be able to help
_____ refuse to trust God with their emotions or neediness
_____ feel angry that God hasn't come through to help them
_____ stay loyal to people and compulsions even when it hurts

Denial

Codependents tend to:
_____ be unaware of their true feelings
_____ deny there is addiction or dysfunction in the family
_____ deny the problems caused by the addiction/dysfunction
_____ minimize or ignore problems in relationships
_____ laugh when they feel like crying
_____ repress emotions, especially negative ones
_____ focus too much on maintaining a good impression
_____ find it hard to express any emotions, even good ones
_____ feel depressed and pretend they aren't depressed
_____ fear their anger and impulses toward revenge
_____ alternate between love/hate toward substance abuser
_____ engage in magical thinking ("it'll all turn out right")
_____ believe all will be well if the other person changes
_____ fear letting themselves be who they are
_____ appear rigid and controlled
_____ mentally "re-stage" events/arguments to turn out better
_____ stay busy so they don't have to think about things
_____ feel confused a lot
_____ substitute spending, eating, etc., for peace of mind
_____ lie to themselves and others
_____ wonder why they feel "crazy" most of the time
_____ refuse to admit shortcomings to self or others
_____ refuse to own their rightful responsibilities

RESIGNED TO HELPLESSNESS

LARGE GROUP

Welcome to the group! For those of you who may be
joining for the first time, the purpose of our meeting
together is to learn about codependency and to escape its
bondage, becoming people who can love others well. We
are beginning to know one another and hoping to learn
to trust each other as the weeks go by. Please take time
during the coming week to familiarize yourself with the "Participation Guidelines"
governing these meetings, found on pages 15-17 of this book.

> **Facilitator:** Read this section aloud. In the rest of this and succeeding sessions, read aloud those sections that are marked for the whole community.
> Ask any new members to introduce themselves to the group by telling their first name. (15 minutes)

During this session we will consider how codependents are resigned to
helplessness. What does that mean? And is that true of you?

Warm-up

1. Choose a partner. Then discuss with him or her what you each learned about
yourself from the assessment you completed.

2. Now imagine that either you or your partner were
assigned to fall backward into the catching arms of the
other. Don't actually *do* the falling, but discuss these
questions with your partner:

> **Facilitator:** You can have the group do the falling exercise instead of just talking about it. However, you do risk injuries if some people are not strong enough to catch their partners. How much do you trust the *physical* strength of your members?

    a. Assuming the catcher was adequately strong,
       which of the two (the faller or the catcher) do you
       think would have the more difficult "task"? Why?

b. Assuming adequate strength, would you be unwilling to do either the falling or the catching? Explain.

c. What does this imagined exercise show you about your attitude toward trust in relationships?

d. Why is trust necessary if this group workshop experience is to be truly helpful?

ON YOUR OWN

Controlled By Others

Read the following section to yourself and put a check next to any sentence or paragraph that describes your own relationship with someone close to you—either past or present. Then write answers to the questions that follow. (15 minutes)

As Jenny sat on the edge of her bed reflecting on the chaos of her life, she sensed she was running out of options. She felt trapped, without choice, compelled to live as she had always lived with Brad. Her absence of choice evidenced itself particularly in two areas: feeling controlled (especially by Brad) and feeling like she had no true self. Both characterize the experience of most codependents.

The first aspect of feeling powerless is our sense of being controlled by someone whose behavior, attitudes, or opinions "make" us do things we don't really want to do. We say things like, "I have to organize my schedule around my children's plans," or "My husband made me lie to his boss," or "I have to bake a casserole for my sick friend." Robbed of options by someone else's real or imagined expectations, we live at the mercy of others' demands and end up feeling used and powerless. We look to others for permission to do something or be someone, and our loss of power results in a profound anger or depression we can neither change nor understand. Without a sense of choice, we codependents feel driven, helpless, and victimized.

The particulars of victimization may vary, but the pattern is predictable. Someone indicates a need by a word, a glance, or a mood, and suddenly we know what must be done: meet that need, no matter what the personal cost in terms of time, energy, even principle. The request or insinuation always takes precedence over our own plans, feelings, or personal agenda. Time and again we comply, the resentment builds, the victim mentality is reinforced, and the sense of powerlessness increases.

It's a vicious cycle, and just telling ourselves to stop doing it isn't enough. The victimization, like the codependency itself, has taken on a life of its own, and it will take an entirely new way of looking at ourselves, of looking at and living life, for us to refuse to be victimized anymore. It will take, in fact, the very power of God.

3. What are some ways you've felt controlled by others' expectations or demands?

4. Tell why you yielded to those expectations or demands. (For instance, what was at stake if you failed to yield?)

5. Think about a time when you felt victimized. What words describe how you felt in that situation? (Perhaps you felt powerless or hateful. Maybe a word picture would describe your feelings: "I felt like a rabbit cornered by a fox," or "I felt like a trampled flower.")

6. How (if at all) did you convey those emotions toward the person responsible for victimizing you?

Read the following section to yourself, again checking anything that relates to your own experience, past or present.
(5 minutes)

ON YOUR OWN

Defined By Others

Feeling powerless isn't just about feeling controlled by others; it's also about feeling like a nonperson. Many of us sense we don't exist at all except as an extension of someone else. We don't know our own thoughts, opinions, or preferences, because we've become too involved in sensing and reacting to other people's thoughts, opinions, and preferences. A codependent friend of mine once turned to her companion in a clothing store and asked, "Do I like this shirt?"

We often let someone else dictate or define who or what we ourselves should be or do. Jenny, for example, would be having a good day until Brad came home in a terrible mood, and then she ended up having a bad day, too. Her personal boundaries in relationship with Brad (the point where her beliefs and feelings ended and Brad's beliefs and feelings began) were blurred, and the two of them had become enmeshed. Finding and being oneself is very difficult for us.

People with blurred boundaries often let others hurt or abuse them. Sexually abused children, for example, believe they have no boundaries, that the doorknob is always on the outside of their door and they have no right to set limits. Who they really are becomes lost in the avalanche of other people's intentions and definitions of who they are. Jenny said nothing if Brad verbally abused her when he was drinking, because she wasn't sure of who she was or what her limits ought to be. She had become so enmeshed with Brad she no longer knew who Jenny was. She sometimes wondered if she existed at all. Only Brad seemed real. His successes were her successes, his failures hers, too. She took his emotional temperature each morning to determine what her own day would be like.

Jenny's absence of choice with regard to Brad was related to her absence of boundaries with regard to herself. She couldn't remember what it was like to do something just for herself. If asked, she would have said doing things for herself felt selfish. Nor did she think she had a right to have her own needs or feelings. Though angry with Brad, Jenny didn't believe her anger had real validity. Accustomed to seeing things only from Brad's point of view, she couldn't admit his drinking was alcoholic, because he didn't see it as alcoholic. Unable to accept her own fear, anger, and despair, Jenny felt she had lost herself and had no idea how to find what she'd lost.

FAMILY GROUP

7. Tell each other how one person (past or present) has power to "make" you do things, sometimes even when you don't really want to.

Facilitator: Form small groups of approximately six persons to discuss questions 7 and 8. If your community is largely the same as last time, keep the same family groups. New people can fill the places left by those who didn't return. If your community has changed greatly, you may need to start groups from scratch.
(15 minutes)

8. Do you want to keep giving that person power to manage your choices? Why do you feel that way?

FAMILY GROUP

Remain with your family group to read aloud the next section and do the exercises that follow.
(20 minutes)

Jesus and Self-Forfeiture

One of the confusing things about codependency is that codependent behaviors often masquerade as Christian virtues. Jesus instructed us to love others as ourselves, to offer the other cheek to those who strike us, to give up our lives, and to sacrifice for others. Is codependency, then, the scriptural norm? Should believers seek to become glad victims of other people's mistreatment?

Let's look at Jesus. Was He codependent? Did He let Himself be controlled by others, a victim without choices? Did He forfeit Himself or sacrifice His personhood when He chose servanthood? Was He defined by other people, taking His identity from what they thought or expected of Him? Were His boundaries blurred so that He allowed His opponents to interfere with His ministry?

9. Read the following passages aloud, one at a time, and discuss how Jesus responded to the control His family and followers tried to exert on Him.

Then Jesus entered a house, and again a crowd gathered, so that he and his disciples were not even able to eat. When his family

30

heard about this, they went to take charge of him, for they said, "He is out of his mind." . . .

Then Jesus' mother and brothers arrived. Standing outside, they sent someone in to call him. A crowd was sitting around him, and they told him, "Your mother and brothers are outside looking for you."

"Who are my mother and my brothers?" he asked.

Then he looked at those seated in a circle around him and said, "Here are my mother and my brothers! Whoever does God's will is my brother and sister and mother."(Mark 3:20-21,31-35)

Jesus began to explain to his disciples that he must go to Jerusalem and suffer many things at the hands of the elders, chief priests and teachers of the law, and that he must be killed and on the third day be raised to life.

Peter took him aside and began to rebuke him. "Never, Lord!" he said. "This shall never happen to you!"

Jesus turned and said to Peter, "Get behind me, Satan! You are a stumbling block to me; you do not have in mind the things of God, but the things of men." (Matthew 16:21-23)

Jesus said, "Have the people sit down." There was plenty of grass in that place, and the men sat down, about five thousand of them. Jesus then took the loaves, gave thanks, and distributed to those who were seated as much as they wanted. He did the same with the fish. . . .

After the people saw the miraculous sign that Jesus did, they began to say, "Surely this is the Prophet who is to come into the world." Jesus, knowing that they intended to come and make him king by force, withdrew again to a mountain by himself. (John 6:10-11,14-15)

After his suffering, [Jesus] showed himself to [the apostles] and gave many convincing proofs that he was alive. He appeared to them over a period of forty days and spoke about the kingdom of God. . . .

So when they met together, they asked him, "Lord, are you at this time going to restore the kingdom to Israel?"

He said to them: "It is not for you to know the times or dates the Father has set by his own authority." (Acts 1:3,6-7)

10. What was Jesus' secret to establishing boundaries? How was He able to clear a path through the jungle of other people's demands? Read the following passage and identify which words or phrases reveal what Jesus knew about who He was in relationship to His Father.

The evening meal was being served, and the devil had already prompted Judas Iscariot, son of Simon, to betray Jesus. Jesus knew

that the Father had put all things under his power, and that he had come from God and was returning to God; so he got up from the meal, took off his outer clothing, and wrapped a towel around his waist. After that, he poured water into a basin and began to wash his disciples' feet, drying them with the towel that was wrapped around him. (John 13:3-5)

11. What does Jesus' self-knowledge tell you about developing your own sense of who you are?

FAMILY GROUP

Prayer Requests

(10 minutes)
Share your prayer requests with others in your small group. Each person can volunteer to pray specifically for one other person during the coming week.

My prayer request is _____

_____

and _____ is praying for me.

I am praying for _____ and his/her prayer request is _____

_____

_____ .

LARGE GROUP

A Word of Hope

(10 minutes)
Once when Jesus visited His good friends Mary and Martha, He found Himself in the middle of a family squabble. Martha complained to Him that her sister Mary was being thoughtless by listening at Jesus' feet instead of helping her. Jesus affirmed Mary's

right to choose to be with Him, and went on to affirm that her choice was a good one. We each have a similar right and responsibility to make choices for ourselves. Listen to Jesus' words:

> **"Martha, Martha, . . . you are worried and upset about many things, but only one thing is needed. Mary has *chosen* what is better, and it will not be taken away from her." (Luke 10:41-42, emphasis added)**

Prayer

All who wish may join in repeating the Serenity Prayer and this familiar version of the Lord's Prayer:

> Lord, grant me the serenity to accept the things I cannot change,
> the courage to change the things I can,
> and the wisdom to know the difference. Amen.

> "Our Father who art in heaven,
>   hallowed be Thy name.
> Thy kingdom come.
> Thy will be done,
>   on earth as it is in heaven.
> Give us this day our daily bread.
> And forgive us our debts,
>   as we forgive our debtors.
> And lead us not into temptation,
>   but deliver us from evil.
> For Thine is the kingdom,
>   and the power, and the glory,
>   forever. Amen."

During the Week

This week keep a list in your journal of the times you feel controlled by someone else. When you have a quiet moment, look over your list and think about whether or not you really had other options in those situations.

For more information on the topic of this session, see *From Bondage to Bonding*, chapter 2. For session 3, see chapter 7.

Benediction

Receive in your hearts these words from the writer of the book of Hebrews:

> **May the God of peace, who through the blood of the eternal covenant brought back from the dead our Lord Jesus, that great Shepherd of the sheep, equip you with everything good for doing his will, and may he work in us what is pleasing to him, through Jesus Christ, to whom be glory for ever and ever. Amen. (Hebrews 13:20)**

Thinking God's Thoughts

Theme for meditation: GOD OFFERS CHOICE.

Reading: Joshua 24:14-24
                    Daniel 1:3-16
                    Psalm 119:97-104
                    Proverbs 4:18-27
                    Matthew 26:36-46
                    Revelation 3:14-20

Prayer:

    Lord, thank You for this evidence in Your Word that You are a God
        who offers us choice:
    Lord, thank You for these areas in my life about which I can make choices:
    Lord, this is one thing I choose to do this week in obedience to Your Word:

FERVENT LONGINGS

Facilitator: Read this section aloud with the entire group.
(5 minutes)

Welcome to this meeting! You have embarked on the rigorous adventure of change and healing from codependency. The pain will be great at times, but so will the blessing. Our faithful, covenant-keeping God offers us His intimate presence as we move into honesty and growth.

Later in this session you will move into family groups of five to seven people. People who are actually related should join different groups. Your group will become your permanent "family" for the remaining weeks of this workshop, and you are encouraged to develop openness and trust with the other members. Each family group can choose its own facilitator.

Warm-up

1. Greet someone you don't know and tell that person why you're here and what you hope will change in your life because of your involvement in this group.

Read the following section individually and write answers to the questions that follow.
(15 minutes)

Built-in Longings

As you enter the path of escape from codependency, you may wonder, "Is it possible to 'recover'? Will I ever be different?" Perhaps you've tried changing your circumstances or "reforming" the people in your life before now and it hasn't worked. Maybe you've even tried unsuccessfully to change yourself. Like any compulsion, codependency doesn't respond to willpower. Behavior adjustments and environmental rearrangements aren't enough. What's needed is a revolutionary new look at what life is and how it's to be lived, particularly in the spiritual dimension.

Let's begin with origins: What are we like as human beings and how did we become codependent? As we understand our bondage, we'll be better equipped to escape it.

The Bible tells us we were created "in the image of God" (Genesis 1:27). That means, among other things, that we're social beings—we long for openness and connectedness with other persons. God is a social Being. He communes in perfect unity within the Godhead (Father, Son, and Holy Spirit), modeling within the Trinity the "society" for which we were created. Our longings for relationships move us toward God and other people.

God always pursues relationship with His image-bearers, just as they long (sometimes unknowingly) for intimacy with Him. God is infinitely desirable; the life Adam and Eve had before they rebelled was a joyous blend of deep pleasure and unabashed dependence on the God from whom their life had come. We all yearn to know and depend on Him.

We're also built to need other people; God gave Adam a helper, even though Adam already had intimacy with Him (Genesis 2:18-25). Our longing for relationship (particularly in the one-woman-one-man covenant for life) is good because it's God-given. Our humanness calls us to mutual interdependence. Adam and Eve were incomplete without each other, and both had the capacity to meet each other's need for help and oneness. We're all made that way.

Before the Fall, Adam and Eve enjoyed both their God-dependence and their mutual interdependence, using their giftedness to bring blessing to God and one another. They also experienced from God and each other what we all long for—to be accepted as we are in any given moment, to be free to not pretend, and to gladly love from a full heart. Their dependencies neither bound nor shamed them. What they had they freely offered, and what they depended on was unfailingly provided—by God and one another.

2. What have been your experiences (if any) of finding God infinitely desirable? Underline whatever you can identify with in these passages.

> **Moses said to him [God], "If your Presence does not go with us, do not send us up from here. How will anyone know that you are pleased with me and with your people unless you go with us? . . ."**
> **And the LORD said to Moses, "I will do the very thing you have asked, because I am pleased with you and I know you by name."**
> **Then Moses said, "Now show me your glory." (Exodus 33:15,17-18)**

O God, you are my God,
  earnestly I seek you;
my soul thirsts for you,
  my body longs for you,
in a dry and weary land
  where there is no water.
I have seen you in the sanctuary
  and beheld your power and your glory.
Because your love is better than life,
  my lips will glorify you. (Psalm 63:1-3)

3. What do you think interferes with your ability to genuinely enjoy God? (It's okay if you don't know.)

4. Choose one adult relationship that is important to you. If you can, tell what you long to give and receive in that relationship. (Children and adolescents view their parents as authority figures, not equals, so this exercise should focus on an adult relationship.)

For example, "From _____ I long to receive _____ [understanding, freedom, listening, intimate discussions, fun together, partnership at tasks, respect, romance . . .]."

Form permanent family groups. The community will now be closed to new participants, so you will be able to build on relationships within your groups.

Let the person who has had the most speeding tickets be the facilitator, unless he or she really doesn't want to. (People who speed tend to be obsessed with time, so this person will keep you on task and on time.) When your groups are arranged, discuss your answers to questions 3 and 4.

(15 minutes)

In your family group, take turns reading paragraphs of the following section aloud and discuss the questions that follow.

(20 minutes)

FAMILY GROUP

Developing Appropriate Dependencies

Unfortunately, Adam and Eve's unfettered relationships in the Garden of Eden didn't last. When they rebelled against dependence on God to become god and goddess of their own lives, they became separated from both the God who had made them and the partners He had made for them (Genesis 3:1-13). It wasn't that their dependencies were removed; they still needed God and each other. But they no longer trusted that those dependency needs would be met. Their longings remained (ours do, too), but without the assurance of being satisfied.

Yet even in a fallen world we're called to appropriate dependencies. Ideally it begins when we, as totally dependent infants, are consistently nurtured by our parents. God intended that our childhood needs be met—not just for physical sustenance but for nurturing as well. Parents should provide love, respect, responsibility, and affirmation, and then help their children transfer their obedience and legitimate dependency needs to God Himself. Thus, as children mature, they move from total dependence on their parents into obedient trust in God and life in community with others—at home, school, church, and neighborhood. The lessons "caught" by the parents' modeling in relationships teach children not how to be autonomous (free from needing others), but how to transfer their legitimate dependence to God and reliable others. The children's dependence is not abandoned but redirected, and mutual interdependence, rather than personal independence, becomes the goal of their maturing process.

Of course, the great difficulty of living in an imperfect world is that as children and as adults we don't consistently experience our need for nurturing being perfectly met—not even with God. It's not God's fault; He's always ready to meet us at every point of need. But as imperfect (even forgiven) human beings our capacity to experience God's acceptance and grace is hindered by nature and by habit.

Nor are there guarantees that our longings for impact, acceptance, and freedom will be met in our relationships with others. In fact, just because we live in a fallen world, we all experience the legitimate fear (even certainty) that our longings for nurturing *won't* be met—certainly not perfectly nor all the time. At best, mutual interdependence is difficult to achieve; at worst, it can be altogether unavailable.

5. Imagine you're a newborn infant who could ask your parents for what you need. Tell the others in your family group what you would say to your parents.

6. Rate the level of nurturing you received as a young child and share your answer with your group. Explain why you chose the rating you did.

0	1	2	3	4	5
I was neglected.					I was nurtured consistently.

7. How do you feel when you think about your answer to question 6?

FAMILY GROUP

Affirming Our Longings

Remain in your famil'
to read aloud the fo'
section. Then discuss the
questions that follow.
(15 minutes)

As we seek to satisfy our deep desire for acceptance and freedom, we must remember that the longings themselves are God-given. A common strategy for avoiding the pain of unmet dependency needs is to stop longing for what we may never receive. It's safer not to need God or others than to face the possibility (even likelihood) that we might not find the love and significance we so desperately crave. Killing our longings for intimate relationships sometimes just seems to make sense.

What we often don't realize, however, is that killing our longings leaves us spiritually closed to connecting with God and others on a level that offers us joy and meaning. When we refuse to feel the ache of our longings, we close the one avenue we have toward having them met.

If there is to be healing from codependency, it must begin by affirming the legitimacy of our longings for acceptance, freedom, and forgiveness in our relationships. Though it will plunge us into the painful reality of those longings having been imperfectly met (or possibly even abused), we must reclaim our birthright of God-dependence and mutual interdependence. If we don't, we may be spared a certain amount of raw pain, but we'll be left hollow at our core and miss the central purpose for which we were created: to love God and others with all our heart, soul, mind, and strength. A deadened heart cannot love or be loved with any integrity at all.

8. To what degree would you say you've deadened your longings for . . .

•intimacy with God?

0	1	2	3	4	5
Not at all					Totally

•intimacy with other people?

0	1	2	3	4	5
Not at all					Totally

9. What does it feel like to have your longings deadened?

The Bible portrays the Lord as a lion:

> **The LORD roars from Zion**
> **and thunders from Jerusalem. (Amos 1:2)**

In C. S. Lewis's book *The Lion, the Witch and the Wardrobe*, we see Jesus pictured as the lion Aslan. When the children in the story first heard about Aslan, they each "felt something jump in his inside."[1] But they each responded differently to the idea of a lion king.

10. When you think of God as a lion, how does that image make you feel? (Do any of the images below come close to your own feelings?)

   a. Like Edmund, who "felt a sensation of mysterious horror"

   b. Like Peter, who "felt suddenly brave and adventurous"

   c. Like Susan, who "felt as if some delicious smell or some delightful strain of music had just floated by her"

   d. Like Lucy, who "got the feeling you have when you wake up in the morning and realise that it is the beginning of the holidays or the beginning of summer"

   e. Other (name it):

11. Tell why you would or would not want your longing for intimacy with God or with others to come alive.

FAMILY GROUP

Prayer Requests
(10 minutes)
Share your prayer requests with other family members. Each person can volunteer to pray specifically for one other person during the coming week.

My prayer request is _____

_____

and _____ is praying for me.

I am praying for _____ and his/her prayer request is _____

_____

_____.

LARGE GROUP

A Word of Hope
(10 minutes)

Jeremiah gave God's words of encouragement to a people separated from God because of their sin—their longings for Him were unmet because they had walked away from Him. Imagine God inviting you into relationship with Himself with these words:

> **"Then you will call upon me and come and pray to me, and I will listen to you. You will seek me and find me when you seek me with all your heart." (Jeremiah 29:12-13)**

Prayer

All who wish may join in repeating the Serenity Prayer:

> Lord, grant me the serenity to accept the things I cannot change,
> the courage to change the things I can,
> and the wisdom to know the difference. Amen.

During the Week

Find thirty minutes or an hour this week to be totally alone. Write in your journal a list of what you long for from God, then write a list of what you long for from the person closest to you. Let yourself feel what it's been like to have had those longings met or unmet. Record your feelings if you can.

Also, take some time to prayerfully consider the covenant agreement at the end of this session. You may wish to fill it in and sign it as your personal commitment to looking honestly at your codependency and at God's blueprint for change with this healing community.

For more information about longings, see chapter 7 of *From Bondage to Bonding*. On losses—the next session's topic—see chapter 8.

Benediction

Listen to the words of the Apostle Jude:

> **To him who is able to keep you from falling and to present you before his glorious presence without fault and with great joy—to the only God our Savior be glory, majesty, power and authority, through Jesus Christ our Lord, before all ages, now and forevermore! Amen. (Jude 24-25)**

Thinking God's Thoughts

Theme for meditation: GOD IS DESIRABLE.

Reading: Exodus 33:12-23
                    Isaiah 26:1-9
                    Psalm 73:21-28
                    Proverbs 3:13-20
                    Luke 9:28-36
                    1 Peter 2:1-7

Prayer:

God, thank You for this evidence in Your Word of how infinitely desirable You are:

God, thank You for these times in my life when I have tasted Your goodness:

God, these are some creative ways I will enjoy You and express my joy in You this week:

NOTE

1. C.S. Lewis, *The Lion, the Witch and the Wardrobe* (New York: Collier Books, 1950), pages 64-65.

Covenant of Commitment
to the Healing Community

Having honestly and prayerfully examined my own style of relating and having found myself in need of facing and changing my codependent strategies for dealing with life, I, _____ (name), do hereby covenant with God that I will do my best to attend meetings of the healing community at _____ (place) on _____ (weekday), and to doggedly pursue self-discovery, self-disclosure, and greater maturity in living the Christian life. My goal throughout this workshop will be to grow in understanding my own character and motivation, to mature in my knowledge of, love for, and dependence on God, and to increase my trust in and mutual interdependence with fellow members of this healing community.

     To that end, I pledge, with God's help, to remain steadfast in my commitment.

Signed this day: _____ (date)

_____ (signature)

(If you sign this covenant, you may wish to seal it by bringing it to the next meeting of your healing community and showing it to the other members of your family group.)

PAINFUL LOSSES

Welcome again to this meeting! Last week we explored the longings we all have to enjoy connectedness with God and others. This week the topic is the losses we all experience from not having our longings fully met.

Warm-up
(5 minutes)
1. Find one member of your family group and briefly tell each other what you learned from writing your "longings list" or from your Bible reading during the week. You may also wish to discuss whether or not (and why) you signed the Covenant of Commitment, found on page 43.

> Join with your family group to read the following section and discuss the questions that follow.
> (30 minutes)

Damage Through Childhood Deprivations
Children come into the world with legitimate yearnings for nurturing they insist others satisfy. Their longings are good, not shameful. However, it's not enough that we simply affirm the appropriateness of our innate longings. We must also face how our dependencies were inadequately met. When the parental bond is missing or weakened, children are damaged.

Sometimes the nurturing loss is extreme; the child's basic physical needs are unmet because of parental addiction or self-centeredness. Equally sad are the homes where abuse occurs: physical (wife-battering and/or child-beating), sexual (physical or verbal), emotional (the child shamed or forbidden to have feelings), or mental (twisting of reality or denial about family secrets). Abused children see themselves as responsible for and deserving of the abuse they receive; guilt, shame, and low self-esteem always characterize these young victims. It can happen in any family, even in a Christian family.

Another way legitimate dependency needs go unmet is when parents abandon children either physically or emotionally. Some parents even use their children to take care of them and their marriages—a devastating kind of role reversal that does great damage. When parents refuse their children the time, attention, and direction they need, those abandoned children suffer profound loss, primarily connected to shame regarding their inner selves. The child's sense of non-worth becomes entrenched when he is unattached to his parents. "If they don't love me," he subconsciously reasons, "I must be unlovable." And the shame, though repressed, follows him into adulthood.

Because children so desperately need nurturing, they will create a fantasy of connectedness with their parents when little or none is available. In the development of codependency, this fantasy bond insulates the codependent from the excruciating pain of reality. The greater the loss of parental bonding, the greater the child's need to pretend it did exist.

The gap in a child's soul resulting from neglect or abuse leaves him feeling that his real self, his inner person, is unacceptable, not enough, inadequate. If he wasn't valued as precious for his own sake, he absorbs the shame of his inadequacy into his deepest image of himself and unintentionally continues to neglect and shame himself even as an adult.

2. Why do you suppose it's often difficult for a person to admit to childhood abuse or abandonment?

3. Did you suffer neglect, abuse, or abandonment as a child? If so, tell your group a little about your experiences.

> Questions 3 and 4 are quite central. If you are under no time constraints, you could spend a whole meeting on these questions and have another meeting for the rest of this session. Also you may want to set an example by giving your own answers to these questions first.

4. How do you think your experiences as a child have affected you as an adult?

Read the next section to yourself and write answers to the questions that follow.
(10 minutes)

Lost Childhood

The loss of adequate parenting in childhood often leaves us as wounded adults with a sense of never having had a childhood at all. Expected to be our own (and sometimes our parents') resource for nurturing, abused or neglected children grow up not knowing how to be genuinely carefree, spontaneous, or free of either parent-imposed or self-imposed responsibilities. We never got to relax and just be children.

Is it any wonder we learned to adapt in order to survive? In the absence of nurturing parents to help us transfer dependency needs to a loving Father God, we survived by depending on ourselves and on others in terribly wrong ways. Soul wounds don't heal if ignored. They shape and govern our emotions, self-images, and relational styles long beyond the childhood in which they were received. We codependents often react out of proportion to the surface significance of an incident because we're living in a different time zone, thrown back emotionally into a childhood situation we felt unable to handle then and thus feel unable to handle as adults. The loss of our childhood has long-term results.

5. Put a mark at the place in this line that best characterizes your childhood. Then explain why you were either over-responsible or carefree.

_____

Burdened and   Carefree
over-responsible   and playful

6. If for the next two months you had total freedom from responsibilities and an unlimited budget, what would you do for fun? How would it make you feel?

7. Name three things you have done just for yourself in the past month. Do you think your amount of personal "play time" was too much, too little, or just right?

FAMILY GROUP

Unacknowledged Losses

Meet with your family group to discuss your answers to the questions above.
(10 minutes)
Remain in your family groups to read the next section and discuss the questions that follow.
(15 minutes)

A child's loss of emotional nurturing often goes unacknowledged, even into adulthood. Codependents cherish an illusion of normalcy about their families of origin, an illusion strengthened by loyalty issues that prevent the "checking out" of childhood experiences. Adults who were not touched, held, rocked, protected, praised, or listened to as children are left with gaps in their souls, and their unacknowledged woundedness usually repeats itself in their relationships with their own children. Nurturing losses are multi-generational.

8. What is one of the most painful losses you can remember experiencing as a child?

9. When did you start acknowledging that as a child you suffered some deeply damaging losses?

10. How have you handled your sense of loss up to now? Is that how you want to continue handling your losses (past and/or present)?

FAMILY GROUP

Prayer Requests

(10 minutes)

Share your prayer requests with other family members. Each person can volunteer to pray specifically for one other person during the coming week.

My prayer request is _____

_____

and _____ is praying for me.

I am praying for _____ and his/her prayer request is _____

_____

_____.

LARGE GROUP

A Word of Hope

(10 minutes)

Though we've all experienced (and still experience) pain from our disappointed longings, yet we can rejoice that God notices our every tear. He told Moses:

> **"I have indeed seen the misery of my people in Egypt. I have heard them crying out because of their slave drivers, and I am concerned about their suffering." (Exodus 3:7)**

God cares about our suffering and stands ready to comfort.

Prayer

Those who wish may repeat the Lord's Prayer:

> "Our Father who art in heaven,
>   hallowed be Thy name.
> Thy kingdom come.
> Thy will be done,
>   on earth as it is in heaven.
> Give us this day our daily bread.
> And forgive us our debts,
>   as we forgive our debtors.
> And lead us not into temptation,
>   but deliver us from evil.
> For Thine is the kingdom,
>   and the power, and the glory, forever. Amen."

During the Week

Record in your journal details about your worst childhood losses, including how you felt and how you dealt with your feelings. (You may want to check with someone who knew you then for accuracy.) Write also how you think those losses and feelings continue to influence your life today.

If this seems like an overwhelming task, start with a list of what you longed for from your mother and father and did not receive.

For more information on this week's topic, see *From Bondage to Bonding,* chapter 8. For more information regarding next week's topic, read chapter 6.

Benediction

Receive these words of comfort from the Apostle Peter:

The God of all grace, who called you to his eternal glory in Christ, after you have suffered a little while, will himself restore you and make you strong, firm and steadfast. To him be the power for ever and ever. Amen. (1 Peter 5:10-11)

Thinking God's Thoughts

Theme for meditation: GOD HEARS OUR PAIN.

Reading: Judges 6:6-16
     Ezekiel 34:7-16
     Psalm 34:11-20
     Proverbs 14:13-14
     John 11:28-36
     Romans 8:22-27

Prayer:
  Lord, thank You for this evidence in Your Word that You hear the pain of
    Your people:
  Lord, thank You for this evidence in my life that You hear my pain:
  Lord, this is what I will do to bring my pain to You:

Childhood Losses

One of the saddest biblical examples of childhood losses is found in the family of King David. Although he was truly a man after God's heart, David failed profoundly to face and deal with the weaknesses of his children.

The unhappy story is recorded in 2 Samuel 13–19. It began when David's eldest son and heir, Amnon, raped his half-sister Tamar, who was probably only twelve to fourteen years old. Disgraced and now unmarriageable, Tamar moved into her brother Absalom's home. Though David her father was furious, he denied the atrocity by neither rebuking nor punishing Amnon for his blatant crime.

But Absalom did not forget. He brooded for two years, planning and then carrying out the murder of Amnon in revenge for his sister's violation. Absalom had to run for his life and remained in exile for three years, hearing nothing from his father David. Again David chose denial and inaction instead of dealing forthrightly with Absalom's murder of Amnon. It was as though Absalom's physical absence from Jerusalem allowed David to close his eyes to the pain of having "lost" both sons. David simply would not look at or deal with the chaos in his family life.

When David finally allowed Absalom to return to Jerusalem, it was two more years before he allowed his son to enter his presence, and then it was without dealing at all with Absalom's sin. Absalom returned unrepentant, bitter about David's failure to deal with Amnon and about his own five-year banishment from his father's presence. The losses of all three of David's children were intensified by the king's utter refusal to deal with the painful realities of their family life.

In the end, David reaped terrible consequences from his denial about his sons' sins. Absalom later attempted a political coup, a civil war fractured the nation, and a second of David's sons met a violent death. The father's refusal to deal with the losses his children suffered proved disastrous for his family and for all Israel.

COMMITTED TO DENIAL

We've examined our legitimate longings to experience intimacy and appropriate dependence on God and others (especially our parents and closest companions). We've also begun to explore the reality that we've all experienced losses from those longings having been unmet or inadequately met in our childhood and in our present circumstances. But those losses are difficult to face, especially because we as codependents are so good at pretending about our feelings. During this session we'll examine the issue of self-deception, or *denial.*

Warm-up
(5 minutes)
1. Greet someone near you and tell why you find it difficult or easy to cry when you feel bad.

> Read the following section to yourself, then write answers to the questions that follow. (15 minutes)

Conspiracy of Silence
Denial is another typical codependent characteristic. Denial in dysfunctional families refers to the refusal to face honestly what *is* in any given situation or relationship—an unwillingness to admit how bad things really are or how bad *we* really are.

Claudia Black, in her book *It Will Never Happen to Me*, describes three unspoken rules of a dysfunctional family: Don't talk; don't trust; don't feel.[1] They are rules about silence, about masking honest appraisals and true feelings regarding what's happening—not just from others, but even from oneself. The "don't talk" rule does great damage, especially to children. Family loyalty becomes synonymous with never discussing or dealing with the family's problems, and the denial sustains and perpetuates the addictive or abusive family system it attempts to protect.

On one level of denial, codependents won't admit they even have problems (or had problems in their families of origin). The drug dependency, mental illness, incest, workaholism, infidelity, or codependency may be obvious to everyone else, but the family members simply refuse to admit anything is abnormal. To them the dysfunctional home is normal, even if miserable.

We codependents also ignore the problems that come from the dysfunction. We engage in magical thinking, the unfounded expectation that the addiction-related difficulties will somehow improve by themselves—the alcoholic will quit drinking, the pornographer will throw away his books and tapes, the daughter will stop bingeing or start eating, the husband will stop beating his wife and kids. The expectation has no basis in reality, but it's part of the denial mechanism.

On a deeper level of denial, we as codependents refuse to face our true feelings. Repression of negative emotions keeps us "safe" from reality and from the frightening consequences of becoming honest. We fear not only the pain of thawing our "frozen feelings," but also the possibility that those emotions would get out of hand if released. We believe our loved ones would surely abandon or abuse us if we ever said how we really feel. It's safer to pretend, to minimize the extent or consequences of the problem, than to risk an honest look at the legitimate grief and anger the problem is causing.

Denial interferes with our relationship with ourselves and with others. In relationship to oneself, denial keeps us from authenticity. We remain strangers to ourselves, unaware of our true feelings and needs and reacting shallowly to even the important people in our lives. We fail to believe or enjoy our own value and impact as persons of worth, and we refuse to genuinely offer our deep selves to others.

Most seriously, when we're not honest about how we've wounded others, including God, our denial keeps us from the intimacy we all long for. We can't share our hearts without knowing our own hearts. Until we reach in to enter our own pain, we can't reach out to share someone else's pain. If we can't be real about our sin, we're blocked from deeply understanding and forgiving others. The basis for genuine intimacy is genuine honesty. Denial sabotages both.

2. What were the "secrets" in your family of origin that no one was allowed to talk about?

3. When, if ever, did you discuss any unhappiness in your family of origin . . .

•with your parents?

•with your brothers and sisters?

•with anyone outside your family?

4. What were (or might have been) the consequences of breaking your family's rule of silence?

5. Think of a relationship that's important to you, and tell how the relationship might change (for better or worse) if you spoke your deepest fears and longings to that person.

FAMILY GROUP

Impression Management

Join your family group and name one of the secrets you listed in question 2. If you are unwilling to do that, explain why. Share with your family group your answer to question 5.
(10 minutes)
Then read this section together and discuss the questions that follow.
(20 minutes)

Denial serves many purposes, but two in particular: projecting a favorable image (especially in the church) and protecting ourselves from the pain of disappointing circumstances and relationships. Let's examine both.

Codependents, like everyone else, want always to look good. Impression management is a top priority for us as we try to convince others our homes are happy and our relationships are functioning well. We're less concerned with how we really feel than with how we ought to feel or how others expect or want us to feel. We pretend we're never too tired, too confused, or too "selfish" to exchange our own needs for someone else's. If we face our true anger, sadness, or resentment, the impression we want to make would suffer and we'd feel ashamed and inadequate. We maintain our false exteriors to sustain our image as competent and loving.

Denial also keeps us from seeing our own love failures. When we face our true emotions, we have to admit our goal is usually self-protection, not ministry. We want to look good more than we want to offer our true selves to others for their good. Impression management is not just deceitful, but unloving.

Another function of denial is to protect ourselves from the pain of an inside look. When we codependents polish the exterior while refusing to examine the interior of our lives, we can avoid for a time the painful reality of what's inside—the character flaws, the disappointment about past or present relationships, the shattered dreams, and the deep loneliness. Denial keeps us from facing that inner pain.

54

6. Do you try to manage how others view you (and how you see yourself)? If so, describe the image you try to portray and live up to.

7. What do Christians especially have to lose by admitting to others the truth about themselves?

8. Read Luke 7:36-50 and tell whether or not Jesus was preoccupied with impression management. What do you think of His behavior?

> Now one of the Pharisees invited Jesus to have dinner with him, so he went to the Pharisee's house and reclined at the table. When a woman who had lived a sinful life in that town learned that Jesus was eating at the Pharisee's house, she brought an alabaster jar of perfume, and as she stood behind him at his feet weeping, she began to wet his feet with her tears. Then she wiped them with her hair, kissed them and poured perfume on them.
>
> When the Pharisee who had invited him saw this, he said to himself, "If this man were a prophet, he would know who is touching him and what kind of woman she is—that she is a sinner."
>
> Jesus answered him, "Simon, I have something to tell you."
>
> "Tell me, teacher," he said.
>
> "Two men owed money to a certain moneylender. One owed him five hundred denarii, and the other fifty. Neither of them had the money to pay him back, so he canceled the debts of both. Now which of them will love him more?"
>
> Simon replied, "I suppose the one who had the bigger debt canceled."
>
> "You have judged correctly," Jesus said.
>
> Then he turned toward the woman and said to Simon, "Do you see this woman? I came into your house. You did not give me any water for my feet, but she wet my feet with her tears and wiped them with her hair. You did not give me a kiss, but this woman, from the time I entered, has not stopped kissing my feet. You did not put oil on my head, but she has poured perfume on my feet. Therefore, I tell you, her many sins have been forgiven—for she loved much. But he who has been forgiven little loves little."
>
> Then Jesus said to her, "Your sins are forgiven."
>
> The other guests began to say among themselves, "Who is this who even forgives sins?"
>
> Jesus said to the woman, "Your faith has saved you; go in peace." (Luke 7:36-50)

9. Why do you suppose Jesus was so unconcerned about what others thought of Him?

FAMILY GROUP

Remain with your family group for the following section.
(20 minutes)

Denial and Spirituality

Denial is not simply a harmless option for dealing with life's problems. The consequences of denial are far-reaching and devastating, especially for our relationship with God. When we cope with life through denial instead of through leaning on God to work through our pain, we remain unconnected to the God we are created to enjoy. Our walk with God thus becomes superficial—we engage in religion instead of enjoying intimate relationship with a personal God. Denial keeps us "safe" from God by keeping us from a desperate dependence on His grace that would deepen our communion with Him. The experience is common to most codependents.

10. While someone from your family group reads aloud these verses, underline any words or phrases that describe how you have felt or perhaps now feel. (Think of "enemy" as anyone who hurts you in some way.)

> **Listen to my prayer, O God,**
> **do not ignore my plea;**
> **hear me and answer me.**
> **My thoughts trouble me and I am distraught**
> **at the voice of the enemy,**
> **at the stares of the wicked;**
> **for they bring down suffering upon me**
> **and revile me in their anger.**
>
> **My heart is in anguish within me;**
> **the terrors of death assail me.**
> **Fear and trembling have beset me;**
> **horror has overwhelmed me.**
> **I said, "Oh, that I had the wings of a dove!**
> **I would fly away and be at rest—**
> **I would flee far away**
> **and stay in the desert;**
> **I would hurry to my place of shelter,**
> **far from the tempest and storm." . . .**
>
> **Let death take my enemies by surprise;**
> **let them go down alive to the grave,**
> **for evil finds lodging among them.**

But I call to God,
    and the LORD saves me.
Evening, morning and noon
    I cry out in distress,
    and he hears my voice.
He ransoms me unharmed
    from the battle waged against me,
    even though many oppose me. (Psalm 55:1-8,15-18)

11. Several group members can share their underlined phrases with everyone.

12. Was David wrong to . . .

- complain to God about his situation? Why, or why not?

- want to run from his problems? Why, or why not?

- want revenge? Why, or why not?

13. Would you feel comfortable telling God . . .

- your negative feelings about your situation? Why, or why not?

- your desire to run away? Why, or why not?

- your desire for revenge? Why, or why not?

14. Would you be willing to share these things with a fellow believer? Explain.

15. What does this psalm teach about how believers ought to talk to God (i.e., pray)?

FAMILY GROUP
Prayer Requests
(10 minutes)
Share your prayer requests with other family members. Each person can volunteer to pray specifically for one other person during the coming week.

My prayer request is _____

_____

and _____ is praying for me.

I am praying for _____ and his/her prayer request is _____

_____

_____.

LARGE GROUP
A Word of Hope
(10 minutes)
David encourages us in Psalm 55 with these words; listen carefully to them:

> **Cast your cares on the LORD**
> **and he will sustain you;**
> **he will never let the righteous fall. (Psalm 55:22)**

Prayer
All who wish may join in repeating the Serenity Prayer:

> Lord, grant me the serenity to accept the things I cannot change,
> the courage to change the things I can,
> and the wisdom to know the difference. Amen.

During the Week
In your journal list three or four things you were not allowed to talk about in your family of origin, or some things you're not allowed to talk about now. Write about how

you felt about those secrets. Find a safe person—perhaps a brother or sister—and talk about one of those secrets this week.

For more information on this week's topic, see *From Bondage to Bonding,* chapter 6. For more information regarding next week's topic, read chapter 11.

Benediction

Hear the words of God through the Apostle Peter:

Grow in the grace and knowledge of our Lord and Savior Jesus Christ. To him be glory both now and forever! Amen. (2 Peter 3:18)

Thinking God's Thoughts

Theme for meditation: GOD VALUES TRUTH.

Reading: Genesis 3:1-13
Isaiah 45:18-25
Psalm 15:1-5
Proverbs 16:13
John 8:31-47
James 5:13-16

Prayer:
Lord, thank You for this evidence in Your Word that You value truth—
    in Yourself and in us:
Lord, thank You for these areas in my life where I've embraced
    and lived out truth:
Lord, this is what I will do (or stop doing) to begin living more
    authentically with You and others:

NOTE

1. Claudia Black, *It Will Never Happen to Me* (Denver, CO: M.A.C. Printing and Publications Division, 1981), chapter 3.

GRIEVING OUR LOSSES

Welcome! During this session we'll consider what we can do about the losses we're willing to acknowledge as we move toward healing from our codependency. This is our sixth week of meeting together, but remember that our process of healing and growth will be life-long. Don't give up. Learn to rest in God.

Warm-up
(5 minutes)
 1. Tell a person near you how you're feeling about yourself since starting this workshop.

> Complete this section on your own.
> (25 minutes)

Grieving Losses
As we face our losses from unmet longings by refusing to stay in denial about our pain, it is important that we seek out a biblical pathway into healing for those losses. The first stage of that healing involves an awakening into grief. Codependents are experts at numbing their souls, and thawing frozen emotions is like warming frostbitten fingers: It hurts. But it's better than gangrene and amputation. The first kind of grief we must experience is mourning our losses—our past and present disappointments in relationships. Losses—even small losses—always require a grieving process.

We codependents begin our grieving process by admitting the damage done to us, particularly in childhood. What others did or failed to do caused us harm, and we must acknowledge the disappointment of our early losses of nurturing and connectedness. *We cannot be healed of the wounds we won't acknowledge.*

We must also grieve our present losses, especially those related to the addiction or compulsion of those close to us. What others are doing to abuse us and what we continue doing as codependents causes enormous damage, and we must mourn our irretrievable opportunities to do one another good instead of harm.

The purpose of facing the pain of our losses is twofold. First, we can't be authentic unless we're honest about the emotional realities of our lives. If we won't face our pain, we'll go on barricading ourselves behind pretense and never achieve openness—an essential element in genuine intimacy.

Second, if we won't face our losses, we can't move beyond them into forgiveness and restoration. Grief opens the door to freedom from past and present damage, with all its hidden angers and subconscious resentments.

Joseph, a victim of abuse at the hands of his brothers, allowed himself to weep repeatedly over their broken relationship. He didn't excuse or minimize their sin, but clearly confronted them with the truth. "You intended to harm me," he told them, "but God intended it for good to accomplish what is now being done, the saving of many lives" (Genesis 50:20). He acknowledged God's sovereign ability to use even their sin to accomplish His good intentions. *Then* Joseph forgave his brothers and "spoke kindly to them" (verse 21). Our honest grieving over our disappointments opens us to the grace we need from God, which we can then, over time, offer to others.

2. Think about what disappointed or wounded you the most in your relationship with your parents. Write a letter to them, saying what you wish you had been able to say to them then.

3. What is one of the greatest disappointments or woundedness in your present life?

4. How are you grieving that loss?

5. Why is it difficult to enter grief over your past and present losses?

With your family group, share something you feel is significant in your answers to questions 2 through 5. Then read and discuss the following section together.
(20 minutes)

FAMILY GROUP

How Should We Grieve?

Children raised in non-nurturing or abusive homes usually find it difficult to grieve their losses authentically. They have for so long repressed or ignored their own feelings that they think they have no feelings at all. How can codependents learn to grieve?

Past pain can sometimes be best entered across the threshold of present relational pain. What is harmful in present relationships likely mirrors what happened in past relationships. By paying attention to how we feel now when we're abused, dismissed, or rejected, we can enter how we felt as children when those things happened to us. When the pain (present or past) comes, we must choose to let it in.

We can also grieve the pain of our losses by seeing how others—a counselor, close friend, or support group member—respond with their own grief to the stories we tell about ourselves. When someone else cries as we recount the sad events of our lives, we can feel a greater depth of sorrow on our own behalf and let our pain in at a deeper level. Over time we'll get better at owning our true feelings even without someone else's affirmation of how we should feel. We can learn to cry for ourselves.

Our grieving will, however, open us to unwelcome emotions like anger and sadness. Especially at first, there may be a welling up of resentment and a desire to alienate ourselves from those who hurt us. This natural reaction ought not to be ignored or repressed, but simply felt. Denial has probably kept these important emotions at bay for years, and by the time they are acknowledged, they are long overdue. Our call is not to act on those negative emotions—by expressing our rage or abandoning relationships, for example—but to be willing to feel them. Grief need not end in resentment or alienation, though it often begins or pauses there on the way to healing.

As we begin to face our losses, we may find within us a deep fear that entering our sorrow or rage might create an emotional avalanche sweeping everything, including ourselves, before it in devastation. Surely we will experience some unsettling and even excruciating emotions along the path to change, but God has promised never to forsake us. His Spirit will strengthen us for whatever we encounter, and His people can support us along the way.

6. What (if anything) frightens or troubles you about the anger that always accompanies loss?

7. Give an example from your own experience of how your anger protects you from the underlying pain of sadness because of a loss.

8. How do the following passages reveal Jesus' attitude toward mourning losses?

> **When Mary reached the place where Jesus was and saw him, she fell at his feet and said, "Lord, if you had been here, my brother would not have died."**
>
> **When Jesus saw her weeping, and the Jews who had come along with her also weeping, he was deeply moved in spirit and troubled. "Where have you laid him?" he asked.**
>
> **"Come and see, Lord," they replied.**
>
> **Jesus wept. (John 11:32-35)**

> **As he approached Jerusalem and saw the city, he wept over it and said, "If you, even you, had only known on this day what would bring you peace—but now it is hidden from your eyes." (Luke 19:41-42)**

> **Then Jesus went with his disciples to a place called Gethsemane, and he said to them, "Sit here while I go over there and pray." He took Peter and the two sons of Zebedee along with him, and he began to be sorrowful and troubled. Then he said to them, "My soul is overwhelmed with sorrow to the point of death. Stay here and keep watch with me."**
>
> **Going a little farther, he fell with his face to the ground and prayed, "My Father, if it is possible, may this cup be taken from me. Yet not as I will, but as you will."**
>
> **Then he returned to his disciples and found them sleeping. "Could you men not keep watch with me for one hour?" he asked Peter. (Matthew 26:36-40)**

FAMILY GROUP

> Remain with your family group for this section.
> (20 minutes)

Comforting Grace

We recovering codependents must grieve our losses, but we are also invited to receive from God's hand grace for dealing with our losses. As we face our past and present pain in relationships, God offers us comforting grace—the Father's gracious presence in the midst of our pain.

When we abandon our denial and begin to face reality without the medicating effect of our former compulsions, we generally expect God will reward us for "being good" by improving our circumstances (or spouse or child or parent). Though the expectation is biblically unwarranted (God didn't make this promise), we count on eventual relief from our pain and are disappointed when that doesn't happen.

What exactly *does* God promise about our pain? Isaiah prophesied that the people of Judah would suffer because of their sin, but in the midst of their suffering God said He would provide what they most needed: His presence.

When you pass through the waters,
   I will be with you;
and when you pass through the rivers,
   they will not sweep over you.
When you walk through the fire,
   you will not be burned;
   the flames will not set you ablaze. . . .
Do not be afraid, for I am with you. (Isaiah 43:2,5)

God's presence offers us a center of comfort in the midst of our storm.

9. What feelings do you have or expect to have as you begin living in less denial about your unmet longings?

10.   a. Which would you prefer: getting rid of the pain, or having God with you in the midst of the pain? Why?

    b. How does this affect your decisions on whether or not to choose codependent strategies for dealing with life?

11. Someone in the group can read aloud these words of David. Then together discuss what words of comfort God might say to you as you grieve your losses.

  As a father has compassion on his children,
    so the LORD has compassion on those who fear him;
  for he knows how we are formed,
    he remembers that we are dust. (Psalm 103:13-14)

12. Would it help you to have comforting hugs of affirmation from the others in your family group? Why, or why not?

FAMILY GROUP

Prayer Requests

(10 minutes)

Share your prayer requests with other family members. Each person can volunteer to pray specifically for one other person during the coming week.

My prayer request is _____

_____

and _____ is praying for me.

I am praying for _____ and his/her prayer request is _____

_____

_____.

LARGE GROUP

A Word of Hope

(10 minutes)

The Apostle John saw a vision of heaven where God "will wipe every tear from [our] eyes. There will be no more death or mourning or crying or pain, for the old order of things has passed away" (Revelation 21:4). Though mourning is an integral part of living in a sinful world, our future as redeemed children of God will turn mourning into song. Praise be to God: Our weeping won't be forever!

Prayer

Those who wish may repeat the Lord's Prayer:

> "Our Father who art in heaven,
>   hallowed be Thy name.
> Thy kingdom come.
> Thy will be done,
>   on earth as it is in heaven.
> Give us this day our daily bread.
> And forgive us our debts,
>   as we forgive our debtors.
> And lead us not into temptation,
>   but deliver us from evil.
> For Thine is the kingdom,
>   and the power, and the glory,
>   forever. Amen."

During the Week

Think of a safe person with whom you could talk about your sorrow over past or present losses. Set a time to talk with that person this week, and pray about whether or not you also need a biblical counselor to help you deal with your feelings.

For more information on this week's topic, see *From Bondage to Bonding,* chapter 11. For more information regarding next week's topic, read chapter 3.

Benediction

Hear the ancient priestly blessing:

> **The LORD bless you**
> **and keep you;**
> **the LORD make his face shine upon you**
> **and be gracious to you;**
> **the LORD turn his face toward you**
> **and give you peace. (Numbers 6:24-26)**

Thinking God's Thoughts

Theme for meditation: GOD COMFORTS HIS CHILDREN.

Reading: 2 Samuel 12:13-25
Isaiah 66:10-13
Psalm 119:49-56
Ecclesiastes 3:1-8
Matthew 5:1-6
2 Corinthians 7:2-7

Prayer:
God, thank You for this evidence in Your Word that You comfort Your children:
God, thank You for these areas in my life where I've experienced Your comfort:
God, this is what I will do (or stop doing) to grieve my losses and to turn to You for comfort:

PART TWO

LAYERS AROUND THE SELF

FEELING WORTHLESS

LARGE GROUP

Welcome! We're in the process of learning about codependency, which has been defined in this way:

> Codependency is a self-focused way of life in which a person blind to his or her true self continually reacts to others, being controlled by and seeking to control their behavior, attitudes, and/or opinions. This results in spiritual sterility, loss of authenticity, and absence of intimacy.

During the past six weeks we have begun looking at some of the losses that undergird our codependency. Turning to face our denial has brought us into grieving the pain we've been running from for so long.

Grieving our losses will probably take a lot longer. We won't put grief aside as we enter the next stage of facing codependency in which we'll look at ways in which we've learned to manage our pain with certain styles of living, certain codependent habits. We'll need the grace of God's presence even more as we continue to uncover broken parts of our hearts.

We've already examined the codependent characteristics of feeling controlled by others and being committed to denial. In this session our focus will be on our tendency to consider ourselves worthless.

Warm-up
(5 minutes)

1. Talk with someone near you about your initial response to today's topic. When someone raises the subject of feeling worthless, what's your first inner reaction?

a. Yes, that's me—worthless!

b. I don't identify with feeling worthless.

c. I'd rather not talk about this.

d. Other (name it):

ON YOUR OWN

Portrait of Self-Contempt

As you read the following section to yourself, circle any words or phrases that describe how you sometimes feel about yourself and/or how you relate to others.
(5 minutes)

Andrea is a social worker responsible for supervising neglected and abused children under state protection. Competent and caring, Andrea is respected by her superiors and by the judges and lawyers with whom she works. Having herself been raised in an abusive home, Andrea takes pride in her ability to help these damaged children, primarily adolescents. Her caseload is heavy to the point of exhaustion, but Andrea never complains; it is another point of personal pride that she can handle the stress of her job.

Because she understands disturbed children, Andrea tends to draw her friendships from people who were themselves abused or neglected. She feels comfortable in the role of helper and avoids relationships with those who aren't needy. Of course, her needy friends end up using her, and Andrea sometimes resents the drain on her time and energy. But her resentment and loneliness are well-kept secrets—even from herself. Andrea would be shocked at the self-disgust and rage beneath her "helper" facade.

People experience Andrea as strong, "together," and a good listener, but not vulnerable or deeply approachable. She never leans on her friends, never outwardly asks anything of anyone. Yet she expects those she helps to feel grateful, admiring, and somehow in awe of her. If they become strong enough not to "need" her, they lose her friendship. Unable to risk not being in charge, Andrea stays one step removed from genuine involvement, except at the level of offering her expertise as counselor. To be needy herself would be not just uncomfortable, but repulsive and even terrifying. She wouldn't say so, but Andrea's deep belief is that she wouldn't be worthwhile or accepted unless she remained in the position of giving help to others.

Codependents don't all look alike. Andrea isn't married to an alcoholic or abuser, like Jenny, but both are codependent. Both are essentially adjusters, people damaged by childhood experiences who cope with their world by trying to please and who end up being controlled instead by others' expectations. Both are desperate for the approval of others and both inwardly despise their inner selves, unable to simply be who they are in their relationships.

FAMILY GROUP

Join your family group and name at least one word or phrase you circled describing yourself. Then answer the following questions.
(15 minutes)

2. Which circled words or phrases would you like to eliminate from your life?

3. Andrea seems like such a caring person. How can you tell that she really despises herself?

If you know each other well enough, you can mention ways you see each other treating yourselves as worthless. Since we codependents usually don't see ourselves clearly, feedback from loving but objective others can be very helpful.

4. What are some things you do because you doubt that who you are is valuable?

FAMILY GROUP

Remain together and take turns reading this section aloud; then discuss the questions.
(20 minutes)

Approval Junkies

An important part of the bondage called codependency is the compulsive need to be approved by others. This need, often unconscious, runs deep and controls virtually every decision we make. Loss of approval feels like death. It is a terrible addiction.

We approval junkies live hostage to other people's opinions and judgments regarding our thoughts, motives, feelings, or behaviors. Enslaved to an insatiable need to be admired, we feel we will cease to exist as persons if others don't affirm us. Though Jenny's appeasing didn't guarantee Brad's affirmation (she couldn't always predict his mood or expectations) and Andrea's "expertise" eventually lost her the close friendships she deeply desired, both codependents nevertheless compulsively sought approval despite the personal cost to themselves. Groveling for affirmation, they were willing to accept mere crumbs even in their most important relationships. At the core of their beings, they felt like zeroes.

Robert McGee in his book on self-esteem, *The Search for Significance*, discusses several lies Satan tells that keep people from experiencing an appropriate self-worth. One lie is, *"I must be approved (accepted) by certain others to feel good about myself."*[1] In other words, we can't have a good self-image unless certain people approve of our attitudes, actions, moods, or personhood. The acceptance must come from the particular person or group we have in mind; anyone else's approval won't satisfy. The approval-giver need not live with or close to us—or even be living at all. Some of us spend our entire lives trying to please a long-deceased mother or father who never approved of us while alive. Approval from beyond the grave is never achievable, but often we compulsively try to earn it anyway.

Approval junkies live with an inordinate fear of rejection. No one likes rejection, but the codependent believes rejection equals death—death to the self, death to any possibility of believing oneself worthwhile. The rejection need not be loud or public; it need not be spoken at all. A word, a glance, a silence, an absence of affirmation—any of those can effectively kill or maim. Often the one withholding the approval knows his or her power to control or punish the one hungry for affirmation, and the dance of manipulation played out between them can be poignantly pathetic. Approval junkies are driven people.

5. Whose approval do you most want to gain? Why is that person's approval important to you?

6. We've called codependency a *self-focused* way of life. Think about desperately seeking approval in order to overcome a feeling of worthlessness. How does this lead to focus on self?

7. How does approval-seeking make it impossible for the codependent to really love other people?

FAMILY GROUP

> Read the following section and discuss the questions together.
> (25 minutes)

I'm Nobody

Though codependents often find themselves in bondage to their desperate fear of rejection, they seldom experience the deep level of approval they crave. In fact, they often end up criticized, demeaned, or disapproved. Consequently, perhaps the most common characteristic of codependents is a low sense of self-worth. Virtually every book written on the subject of codependency includes a section on poor self-esteem.

Codependents often grew up in homes where children and their needs were considered worth less than something else—alcohol, drugs, sexual satisfaction, the neighbors' (or deacons') opinion, convenience, making money, keeping peace in the family, time with friends, and so on. When a child is consistently given a low priority, he brings into adult life a belief that he is unworthy of love and esteem, especially if he has failed to measure up to the performance expected of him.

The conspiracy against self-valuing is heightened by our culture's notion that only the rich, bright, good-looking, productive, successful, or popular are worthwhile. Those who don't measure up should be ignored, punished, or ostracized. As Robert McGee wrote, a lie Satan wants us to believe is, *"Those who fail are unworthy of love and deserve to be punished."*[2] Codependents who sense they are not worth much also believe they deserve whatever bad treatment other people hand out—it's what they have coming. The expectation of abuse goes hand in hand with low self-esteem.

Thus, Jenny, for example, felt she didn't really deserve a happy home or kind treatment from her husband and children; after all, she hadn't always been the perfectly loving wife and mother she wanted to be and had always tried to be. She believed the lie: *Those who fail are unworthy of love.* She didn't deserve to be happy; she should have tried harder.

People with low self-esteem participate in their own mistreatment through self-destructive behaviors consistent with their deep sense of inferiority. Codependents feel trapped by past failures and doomed to repeat those failures in the future. Their self-contempt can be verbal or behavioral, announcing to the world, "I don't deserve anything good because I'm worthless. I don't blame you for not liking me; I don't like me, either." Often it's merely internal—the negative sentences we say to ourselves about ourselves in our quiet moments.

However self-contempt is lived out, it's an expression of the belief that our personhood is hopelessly flawed and unchangeable. Whether by word, action, or inaction, we hold ourselves in contempt by pursuing habitually destructive patterns that keep us bound to our own low view of our worth.

Self-contempt easily becomes self-neglect—sometimes mild (like feeling guilty for spending time just for ourselves), sometimes severe (like refusing to see a doctor about an ailment because we don't feel worthy of the cost of treatment). Some codependents allow themselves to be repeatedly abused because they hate themselves. If followed to its logical conclusion, self-neglect can lead to attempts at suicide, or perhaps the more subtle "slow suicide" of disorders like anorexia, drug addiction, or alcohol abuse. Self-contempt is more than just a poor choice of attitude; it can endanger one's very life.

8.   a. Do you identify with the lie, "Those who fail are unworthy of love"? Explain.

b. How do you think you started believing that lie?

c. Who or what encourages you to believe that lie today?

The Bible says God values us enough to suffer for us, even if we've failed to live up to His or our standards. The apostle Paul said,

God demonstrates his own love for us in this: While we were still sinners, Christ died for us. (Romans 5:9)

9. Why do you suppose it's so hard for us to relax in the knowledge that we are loved failures? If God isn't pushing us to measure up, what is?

The news about him [Jesus] spread all the more, so that crowds of people came to hear him and to be healed of their sicknesses. But Jesus often withdrew to lonely places and prayed. (Luke 5:15-16)

10. Do you think Jesus was selfish to withdraw regularly from hurting people to serve His own need to be alone with His Father? Why do you feel that way?

11. How easy is it for you to need God so much that you have to say no to people often in order to be with Him? Why do you suppose that is?

FAMILY GROUP

Prayer Requests
(10 minutes)
Share your prayer requests with other family members. Volunteer to pray specifically for one other person during the coming week.

My prayer request is _____

_____

and _____ is praying for me.

I am praying for _____ and his/her prayer request is _____

_____

_____.

LARGE GROUP

A Word of Hope
(10 minutes)
Jesus expected people to love and value themselves, just as He valued Himself. If we don't esteem ourselves, we can't properly obey God's command to love others well.

As an encouragement to greater self-esteem, listen to these words of Jesus about the second greatest commandment:

> **"Love your neighbor as yourself." (Matthew 22:39; cf. Leviticus 19:18)**

Prayer

All who wish may join in repeating the Serenity Prayer, found on page 58.

During the Week

This week write in your journal several ways your low self-esteem might "benefit" you. In other words, what might be expected of you if you felt a high level of self-esteem that you wouldn't have to take responsibility for as a "nobody"? Write your conclusions and share them with another person from the group before the next meeting.

For more information on this week's topic, see *From Bondage to Bonding,* chapter 3. For more information regarding next week's topic, read chapter 9.

Benediction

Listen to the words of the Apostle Jude:

> **To him who is able to keep you from falling and to present you before his glorious presence without fault and with great joy—to the only God our Savior be glory, majesty, power and authority, through Jesus Christ our Lord, before all ages, now and forevermore! Amen. (Jude 24-25)**

Thinking God's Thoughts

Theme for meditation: GOD VALUES ME.

Reading: Genesis 1:26-31
                      Isaiah 43:1-7
                      Psalm 139:13-18
                      Proverbs 15:26
                      John 15:9-17
                      Revelation 5:6-10

Prayer:
        God, thank You for this evidence in Your Word that You value me:
        God, thank You for this evidence in my own life that I am dear to Your heart:
        God, here are some creative ways for me to show that I agree with You that
                I am precious:

NOTES

1. Robert S. McGee, *The Search for Significance* (Houston, TX: Rapha Publishing, 1987), page 30.

2. McGee, page 68.

Timothy's Self-Esteem

Timothy grew up in a little town called Lystra. His mother was Jewish and raised him to believe in the Jewish God. But his father was Greek. Greeks found the Jewish custom of circumcision disgusting, so Timothy's father drew the line at allowing that to be done to his son.

Consequently, the teenage Timothy was neither fish nor fowl. Because of his beliefs and habits, Greeks regarded him as a Jew, but the Jews considered him a Greek because he wasn't circumcised. When a Jew named Paul arrived in town and announced that the Jewish Messiah had come and welcomed anyone who would serve Him, circumcised or not, this was great news to Timothy. He became a passionate follower of Christ and eventually joined Paul's missionary team.

We don't know all the pain Timothy experienced as a child, but certainly his youthful identity crisis must have hurt. And the effects of his wounds did not disappear overnight once he committed himself to Christ. Years later, when Timothy was a fruitful leader, Paul was still encouraging him not to fall back into old patterns. Timothy tended to accept others' scorn for him, but Paul wrote,

> **Don't let anyone look down on you because you are young, but set an example for the believers in speech, in life, in love, in faith and in purity. . . . Do not neglect your gift, which was given you through a prophetic message when the body of elders laid their hands on you. (1 Timothy 4:12,14)**

> **God did not give us a spirit of timidity, but a spirit of power, of love and of self-discipline.**
> **So do not be ashamed to testify about our Lord, or ashamed of me his prisoner. (2 Timothy 1:7)**

FALSE SELVES

LARGE GROUP

Welcome! In this meeting we'll share more of ourselves as we look beneath the surface of our lives. Just a reminder: In groups such as these, confidentiality must be the hallmark of our self-disclosure time. What is said to one another individually and in the group setting must not go beyond these walls. It stays here and in our minds as we pray for one another throughout the week.

Warm-up
(5 minutes)
 1. Turn to someone and tell each other one thing you've learned about yourself in the last seven weeks that you want God to change and why.

ON YOUR OWN

> Read this section to yourself and write answers to the questions that follow.
> (15 minutes)

Abandoning the True Self
Consider the dilemma of Randy, a young boy of eleven. He is bright, mildly dyslexic, athletic, rather shy. His parents separated when he was seven. His mother left with another man after Randy's father had beaten her "for the last time." When she finally returned, Randy's father left town; they haven't seen him since.

Randy was battered physically and verbally by his father, whose raging temper intensified when he drank. The abuse left the child angry, fearful, guilt-ridden, and deeply lonely. Hungry for affection and shamed for being what normal boys are, Randy learned early it wasn't safe being Randy. He would have to become someone else to avoid future abuse. Believing himself unlovable because of his parents' abandonment and abuse, he layered over the precious child within (his unique personality and true feelings) with a mask of indifference and eventually rebellion.

Already at age eleven Randy was a classic codependent. He felt controlled and without boundaries, and he felt contempt for himself because of the abandonment. He clung to denial by refusing to believe things were as bad as they were, even bragging he could whip anyone because no kid could hurt him as much as his dad did. He was committed to trying to control his world and the people in it, and he worked hard to be self-sufficient, taking an extensive paper route at age eight so he wouldn't have to depend on anyone. Unconsciously and of necessity, Randy learned to survive by becoming something other than the carefree, spontaneous, loved, disciplined, precious eleven-year-old he wanted to be and ought to have been.

2. What feelings did you have as you read Randy's story? Why?

3. Do you identify with any of Randy's losses or longings? Which ones?

Meet together to discuss the
next section.
(15 minutes)

False Selves

Children growing up in dysfunctional homes frequently learn to create a self that can survive the trauma of neglect or abuse. Children of alcoholics, for example, adopt predictable and compulsive roles to cope with their chaotic family life—the hero, the scapegoat, the lost child, or the mascot. The primary reason a child adopts a role is to please or appease his parents. Being himself hasn't worked, so he tries another tack—becoming another kind of child who might deserve to be loved. Randy was abandoned, not cherished; battered, not protected; demeaned, not affirmed. But perhaps (he unconsciously concluded) he might get what he longed for if he were good enough, industrious enough, helpful enough. And if that didn't work, he could rebel, acting out his anger to perversely justify his parents' treatment of him as worthless.

Another function of the false self is to avoid the pain and anger the child feels but dares not acknowledge, even to himself. Randy may be raging on the inside, but to stay safe from his father he'd better not rage on the outside. Being "nice" keeps him out of pain better than being "real," so that's what he's become, though his camouflaged belligerence occasionally explodes. Randy will probably grow up angry with the world, yet committed to never making waves with anyone, even if he has to sacrifice his emotional integrity in the process. Other abused children may do penance, make jokes, run away, hurt another child (or a pet)—anything that works to muffle or lessen their inner terror and anger.

Roles are not thoughtfully evaluated and deliberately chosen, like picking a Halloween mask from the toy store shelf. Abused, neglected children just become whatever "works" to help them survive, and the false self is carried into all their adult relationships.

4. What image do you project to the world that you want others to believe is true about you?

5. What longings and/or losses do you suppose led you to take on that particular image?

6. What purpose do you think this image serves for you? (Consider what Randy's image achieved for him.)

FAMILY GROUP

Discuss the next section together.
(30 minutes)

Blocked from Loving Others

One of the wonderful things about the pre-Fall relationship between Adam and Eve was their ability to live totally open and unprotected, both physically and personally. What they'd been given by God—their unique personalities, gifts, and talents—they enjoyed and offered to one another in glad other-centeredness. Contrast that with the self-focused codependent. Control, self-sufficiency, self-protective denial—codependents care less about loving others than about making up for their childhood losses by getting their own needs met. Dysfunctional people who live behind layers are self-preoccupied, not other-centered. Even their giving is designed to assure that they're getting something in return.

Moreover, we codependents cannot give what is essential to love because we haven't learned to receive it ourselves: freedom to allow others to be who they are. Because of our own bondage to self, we can't offer forgiveness and grace to the imperfect people who occupy our lives. Codependency constitutes a deep failure to love, a failure for which God holds us accountable and for which Christ had to die on our behalf.

Jesus was outspoken in His criticism of pretense, particularly among the religious leaders of His day, the Pharisees.

Take turns reading paragraphs of the passage below.

> **Then Jesus said to the crowds and to his disciples: "The teachers of the law and the Pharisees sit in Moses' seat. So you must obey them and do everything they tell you. But do not do what they do, for they do not practice what they preach. They tie up heavy loads and put them on men's shoulders, but they themselves are not willing to lift a finger to move them.**
>
> **"Everything they do is done for men to see: They make their phylacteries wide and the tassels on their garments long; they love the place of honor at banquets and the most important seats in the synagogues; they love to be greeted in the marketplaces and to have men call them 'Rabbi.' . . .**
>
> **"Woe to you, teachers of the law and Pharisees, you hypocrites! You give a tenth of your spices—mint, dill and cumin. But you have neglected the more important matters of the law—justice, mercy and faithfulness. You should have practiced the latter, without neglecting the former. You blind guides! You strain out a gnat but swallow a camel.**
>
> **"Woe to you, teachers of the law and Pharisees, you hypocrites! You clean the outside of the cup and dish, but inside they are full of greed and self-indulgence. Blind Pharisee! First clean the inside of the cup and dish, and then the outside also will be clean.**
>
> **"Woe to you, teachers of the law and Pharisees, you hypocrites! You are like whitewashed tombs, which look beautiful on the outside but on the inside are full of dead men's bones and everything unclean. In the same way, on the outside you appear to people as righteous but on the inside you are full of hypocrisy and wickedness." (Matthew 23:1-7,23-28)**

7. How would you summarize Jesus' attitude toward pretense?

8. How does reading Jesus' words about the Pharisees make you feel?

a. I feel guilty of hypocrisy and condemned.

b. I feel guilty of hypocrisy but grateful for God's forgiveness.

c. I despise myself.

d. I want to stop being hypocritical.

e. I don't identify with the Pharisees at all.

f. Other (name it):

9. Read aloud these passages, and tell what the Bible says God feels about the real you, the inner person you are. Which phrases do you most long to hear God say about you?

> **O LORD, you have searched me**
> **and you know me.**
> **You know when I sit and when I rise;**
> **you perceive my thoughts from afar.**
> **You discern my going out and my lying down;**
> **you are familiar with all my ways.**
> **Before a word is on my tongue**
> **you know it completely, O LORD. . . .**
>
> **For you created my inmost being;**
> **you knit me together in my mother's womb.**
> **I praise you because I am fearfully and wonderfully made;**
> **your works are wonderful,**
> **I know that full well.**
> **My frame was not hidden from you**
> **when I was made in the secret place.**
> **When I was woven together in the depths of the earth,**
> **your eyes saw my unformed body.**
> **All the days ordained for me**
> **were written in your book**
> **before one of them came to be. (Psalm 139:1-4,13-16)**
>
> **You see, at just the right time, when we were still powerless, Christ died for the ungodly. Very rarely will anyone die for a righteous man, though for a good man someone might possibly dare to die.**

But God demonstrates his own love for us in this: While we were still sinners, Christ died for us. (Romans 5:6-8)

10. How easy is it for you to believe you are that special and precious to God? Why?

11. Psalm 139 makes it clear that God knows everything about you. Is that good news for you or scary news? Explain.

FAMILY GROUP

Prayer Requests
(10 minutes)
Share your prayer requests with other family members. Volunteer to pray specifically for one other person during the coming week.

My prayer request is _____

_____

and _____ is praying for me.

I am praying for _____ and his/her prayer request is _____

_____

_____.

LARGE GROUP

A Word of Hope
(10 minutes)
Jesus spoke many "woes" to the Pharisees for their pretense, but His heart motivation was love—He longed to draw them to Himself in repentance and faith. Listen to His words at the close of His criticism of the Pharisees:

"O Jerusalem, Jerusalem, you who kill the prophets and stone those sent to you, how often I have longed to gather your children together, as a hen gathers her chicks under her wings, but you were not willing." (Matthew 23:37)

God exposes our own pretense for the same loving reason: He longs to bless us, if only we will repent and open our inner selves to Him.

Prayer

Those who wish may repeat the Lord's Prayer, found on page 66.

During the Week

Ask the Holy Spirit to reveal your pretense to you this week. Keep a list in your journal of the times you "fake it," and jot down how the pretense "benefited" you in the moment.

For more information on this week's topic, see *From Bondage to Bonding,* chapter 9. For more information regarding next week's topic, read chapter 4.

Benediction

Receive these words of comfort from the Apostle Peter:

The God of all grace, who called you to his eternal glory in Christ, after you have suffered a little while, will himself restore you and make you strong, firm and steadfast. To him be the power for ever and ever. Amen. (1 Peter 5:10-11)

Thinking God's Thoughts

Theme for meditation: GOD KNOWS OUR TRUE SELVES.

Reading: 1 Samuel 16:1-7
Jeremiah 1:4-10
Psalm 139:1-6
Proverbs 24:12
Mark 9:33-37
Hebrews 4:12-16

Prayer:
Lord, thank You for this evidence in Your Word that You know all things:
Lord, thank You for this evidence in my life that You love me, even knowing everything about me:
Lord, this is how I will open myself to You so You can reveal to me what I don't yet know about myself:

Faking It

Ananias and Sapphira belonged to the group in Jerusalem who believed that Jesus of Nazareth had proven Himself to be the Messiah by rising from the dead. Those Jews who believed in Jesus' resurrection were a tight-knit community pushing against the tide of the majority Jewish opinion. They were so committed to each other that they treated one another like family, even selling property to feed and clothe their poorer brothers and sisters.

Ananias and Sapphira wanted the community to approve of them. They wanted to appear to be as generous as the others. But they were afraid to lose all of their assets; they wouldn't feel comfortable without a little nest egg. So they sold a piece of property, but they lied to the community's leaders about the price. They claimed to give the entire sum for their poor fellow believers, but actually they kept back a portion.

Peter challenged their hypocrisy. No one had pressured them to sell their property; that pressure had come only from their desire to appear generous and win approval. No one had compelled them to donate the entire sum. God was not angry that they wanted to keep some investments, but He was incensed that they lied to project a false image of themselves. The minute the lie left each of their lips, they each dropped dead. God wanted to make it absolutely clear that His people were free to progress slowly and to struggle with doubts and fears, but they were not free to pretend to be holier than they were. (See Acts 5:1-11.)

DESPERATE TO CONTROL

LARGE GROUP

During the past eight sessions we've looked at several characteristics of codependency—self-focusing, denial, and low self-esteem, for example. The codependent despises his inner self and gives up control of his life to others, yet strangely, he does it all for himself. And behind his feeling that he is at the mercy of others' whims lies another trait: a desperate intention to control his world. That need to control is the topic of this week's session.

Warm-up
(5 minutes)

1. Meet with two other people near you and discuss the last session's "homework" assignment. What were some instances during the week when you used your "false self" to stay safe from others emotionally?

ON YOUR OWN

> Read this scenario to your-
> self and write answers to the
> questions that follow.
> (10 minutes)

What if . . . ?

Carol and Tom are coworkers in an airline-related industry. Their jobs put them in contact with pilots from many different airlines, and they both know some of those pilots socially as well as professionally. One pilot in particular had become a favorite, a man well-liked for his charm and sense of humor. Phil had flown for years with a mostly unblemished record, even though during his off-hours he was known to sometimes over-indulge in alcohol.

One afternoon Phil was called in as an emergency substitute for a pilot whose son had been injured in a serious automobile accident. Carol and Tom had had lunch with Phil that day, and they had commented to each other afterward that Phil must have started drinking early to have been as "happy" as he was that noon—even before his lunch martinis. They liked Phil a lot, but when they found out he was scheduled to fly that afternoon, they exchanged glances of genuine concern. What about the lives of the passengers on Phil's plane? Both Carol and Tom had access to Phil and to the officials of his airline, and both knew Phil's wife, Janet.

2. If you were Carol or Tom, what would you do?

3. Why would you take that action?

4. What, if anything, would you do if you were Janet?

FAMILY GROUP

Meet together for this section.
(30 minutes)

The Compulsion to Control

Though we codependents typically experience a strong sense of being controlled or victimized by others, we also try desperately to control the actions or moods of those we care about. We're determined to ensure the "good" behavior of our spouse, parent, child, or friend ("good" defined as sober, straight, law-abiding, nonviolent, etc.). Our control efforts reflect our belief that we're more powerful than we really are because we don't want to face our actual sense of powerlessness. One form of control is known in the addiction recovery field as *rescuing*.

Rescuing is what a person does to save others from the negative consequences of their choices. Sometimes codependents rescue by doing something they should not do. When Jenny went downtown to bring Brad home from his drinking binge, she was rescuing. Sometimes a rescue involves failing to do what we ought to do. Parents who won't hold a child responsible to pay for what he broke or lost are rescuing that child from accountability. Rescuing intends to save the pride, comfort, reputation, job, or finances of the "rescuee." Codependents feel they owe it to the ones they love.

Another common control mechanism is *caretaking*. Caretaking is what we do for others that they could and should do for themselves. We codependents "take over" the responsibility for others' choices, operating on the assumption that our way is the only right way. The person at the receiving end of our caretaking is assumed to be incompetent to accomplish the task at hand successfully. We tell our spouses which traffic lane to drive in or what the speed limit is; we follow behind our children, making sure they do things right the first time; we tell our friends exactly what we want them to do so we won't be disappointed. We insist on preventing other people's mistakes.

To be fair, sometimes a lot is riding on it. Sometimes the stakes involve the survival of a job or a reputation or a relationship. For instance, when a woman stops telling her husband how to manage his job, he might, in fact, lose his job—and their financial security. If a man stops checking up on his wife as a way to keep her faithful, she might move in with her lover. When a wife stops acting as though her husband's emotional equilibrium is her responsibility, she may face divorce. These are high stakes, and somehow caretaking, even if it's patronizing, seems a very attractive alternative.

5. Which of the "solutions" you suggested to Carol and Tom's dilemma would qualify as a codependent "rescue" of Phil?

6. Are you rescuing or caretaking anyone close to you? Tell the group about that.

7. Why should we stop our strategies of rescuing or caretaking (controlling what others do) if the consequences can be so terrible? Is control preferable to disaster?

8. What "side benefits" might you achieve by staying in control (through both rescuing and caretaking)?

9. Did Jesus rescue people from the consequences of their choices or do things for them that they could have done? Consider the following passages.

> **On hearing it [Jesus' words about himself], many of his disciples said, "This is a hard teaching. Who can accept it?"**
>
> **Aware that his disciples were grumbling about this, Jesus said to them, "Does this offend you? What if you see the Son of Man ascend to where he was before! The Spirit gives life; the flesh counts for nothing. The words I have spoken to you are spirit and they are life. Yet there are some of you who do not believe." For Jesus had known from the beginning which of them did not believe and who would betray him. He went on to say, "This is why I told you that no one can come to me unless the Father has enabled him."**
>
> **From this time many of his disciples turned back and no longer followed him.**
>
> **"You do not want to leave too, do you?" Jesus asked the Twelve.**
>
> **Simon Peter answered him, "Lord, to whom shall we go? You have the words of eternal life. We believe and know that you are the Holy One of God." (John 6:60-69)**

> **Jesus was troubled in spirit and testified, "I tell you the truth, one of you is going to betray me."**
>
> **His disciples stared at one another, at a loss to know which of them he meant. One of them, the disciple whom Jesus loved, was reclining next to him. Simon Peter motioned to this disciple and said, "Ask him which one he means."**
>
> **Leaning back against Jesus, he asked him, "Lord, who is it?"**
>
> **Jesus answered, "It is the one to whom I will give this piece of bread when I have dipped it in the dish." Then, dipping the piece of bread, he gave it to Judas Iscariot, son of Simon. As soon as Judas took the bread, Satan entered into him.**
>
> **"What you are about to do, do quickly," Jesus told him, but no one at the meal understood why Jesus said this to him. Since Judas had charge of the money, some thought Jesus was telling him to**

buy what was needed for the Feast, or to give something to the poor. As soon as Judas had taken the bread, he went out. And it was night. (John 13:21-30)

10. What did refusing to rescue or caretake cost Jesus?

ON YOUR OWN

Control as Failure to Love

Read this section to yourself and put a check near the words or phrases that describe your own strategies of control. Then write answers to the questions. (10 minutes)

One reason rescuing and caretaking are so destructive is that they violate the freedom God created us to enjoy as His image-bearers. Though rescuing, for example, feels heroic to the rescuer, it robs the "rescuee" of the self-respect that comes from knowing his or her choices matter because those choices have consequences. A rescuer gives the message: "Be foolish if you want; I'll be the strong one to save you from yourself." By allowing the rescue, the workaholic or alcoholic or rebellious child ends up feeling incompetent, babied, and furious.

Caretaking also sabotages our God-given freedom. Gerald May says, "God lets us make our own decisions, even at times when we would much prefer to be taken care of. God blesses us with responsibility and the dignity it contains."[1] In contrast, we codependents undermine the competence and accountability of those we try to control, and it ought not surprise us when others resent the manipulation. Control sabotages healthy give-and-take in relationships, swinging power and responsibility toward one partner and leaving the other feeling managed, unfree, and angry.

Real or imagined control provides us with a temporary feeling of strength, superiority, and indispensability—a kind of "savior" identity. The hidden payback of feeling "in charge" as savior actually feels quite good to us. People see us as the poor suffering martyr, the only "good guy" in the situation, casting everyone else into the villain role. It's a compulsive and unloving "benefit."

11. What specific payback do you receive or expect in exchange for your attempts to control the people and circumstances of your life?

12. What do you think would happen if you were to *stop* the control strategies you know you practice?

13. Why would that be unacceptable to you or to those you love?

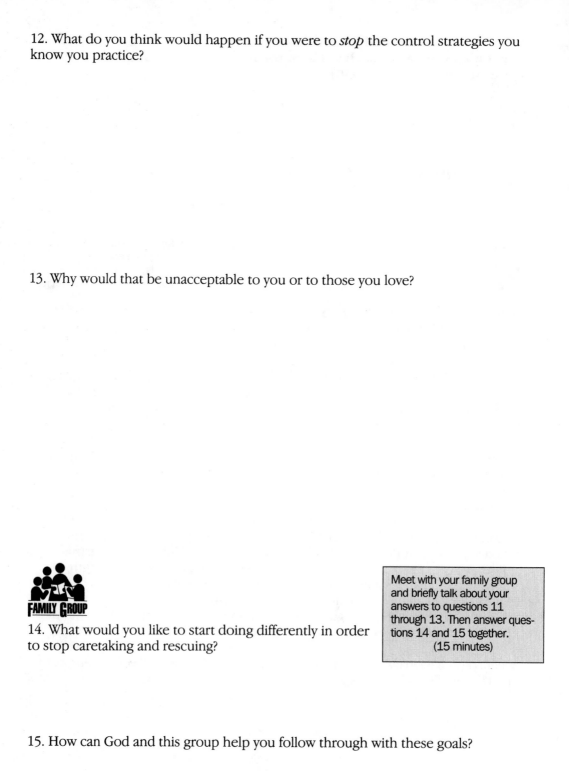

FAMILY GROUP

14. What would you like to start doing differently in order to stop caretaking and rescuing?

Meet with your family group and briefly talk about your answers to questions 11 through 13. Then answer questions 14 and 15 together. (15 minutes)

15. How can God and this group help you follow through with these goals?

Prayer Requests

(10 minutes)

Share your prayer requests with other family members. Volunteer to pray specifically for one other person during the coming week.

My prayer request is _____

_____

and _____ is praying for me.

I am praying for _____ and his/her prayer request is _____

_____

_____.

A Word of Hope

(10 minutes)

Instead of fearfulness regarding our circumstances, we can be encouraged by the words of the psalmist:

> **Trust in the LORD and do good;**
> **dwell in the land and enjoy safe pasture.**
> **Delight yourself in the LORD**
> **and he will give you the desires of your heart. (Psalm 37:3-4)**

Prayer

All who wish may join in repeating the Serenity Prayer.

During the Week

Record in your journal situations that tempt you to rescue or take care of someone. Write why you want to control the situation and how you feel about doing or not doing that.

For more information on this week's topic, see *From Bondage to Bonding,* chapter 4. For more information regarding next week's topic, read chapter 9.

Benediction

Hear the words of God through the Apostle Peter:

> **Grow in the grace and knowledge of our Lord and Savior Jesus**
> **Christ. To him be glory both now and forever! Amen. (2 Peter 3:18)**

Thinking God's Thoughts

Theme for meditation: GOD OFFERS FREEDOM.

Reading: Genesis 2:15-17
1 Samuel 2:22-30
Psalm 51:1-12
Proverbs 19:13,19
Mark 10:17-22
Galatians 5:13-15

Prayer:
God, thank You for this evidence in Your Word that You are a God who
offers us freedom:
God, thank You for these areas in my life where I can offer freedom to others:
God, this is what I will do (or stop doing) to allow someone close to me
freedom and responsibility:

NOTE

1. Gerald May, *Addiction and Grace* (San Francisco, CA: Harper & Row, Publishers, 1988), pages 120-121.

SELF-PROTECTION

You're to be congratulated on your faithfulness in coming to this group week after week. It speaks of your intention to face even the painful things in your life and to seek the help of God and other people to make difficult choices to change. May the Father bless your commitment!

Warm-up
(5 minutes)
 1. Greet someone close to you and tell each other the funniest thing that happened to you during the past few weeks. If nothing is feeling funny these days, give yourself permission to say so, and ask for a hug.

> Read this section to yourself
> and write answers to the
> questions that follow.
> (20 minutes)

Misplaced Dependencies
Children growing up in neglectful or abusive families unconsciously compensate for their losses by turning to wrong sources for getting their dependency needs met. Instead of being nurtured by parents and taught to transfer their dependence to God and trustworthy others, uncherished children often grow to choose mood-altering substances (alcohol, drugs, etc.) or compulsions (like gambling, shopping, overeating, perfectionism, working, etc.) to dull their pain for a time. Many become trapped in relational bondage like codependency, pursuing the seductive hope that "fixing" others will somehow restore damaged relationships. False dependencies—addictions, compulsions, codependency—become the wounded child's protection against past and present disappointments. In a culture accustomed to instant relief for every ailment, the substances, habits, and relationships that keep emotional pain at arm's length work well to medicate our unhappiness.

Self-protection keeps us in control of our lives, or at least it affords the illusion of control. We're determined to prevent a repeat of earlier losses, never to be hurt again. Wrong dependencies provide predictable (though temporary) relief and a comforting (though false) sense of power. Codependents consider self-protection perfectly reasonable.

2. Do you think pain relief has been a high priority for you? Explain.

3. Why do you suppose God is less committed to our pain relief than we are?

4. Look back at your Personal Assessment on pages 23-25 and name one or two of your most dominant codependent character traits. Then tell how they protect you in relationships.

Read these prophecies from Isaiah and Jeremiah, in which God compares self-protection to lighting a fire and digging a well.

> **Who among you fears the LORD**
> **and obeys the word of his servant?**
> **Let him who walks in the dark,**
> **who has no light,**
> **trust in the name of the LORD**
> **and rely on his God.**
> **But now, all you who light fires**
> **and provide yourselves with flaming torches,**
> **go, walk in the light of your fires**
> **and of the torches you have set ablaze.**
> **This is what you shall receive from my hand:**
> **You will lie down in torment. (Isaiah 50:10-11)**

> **[The Lord said,] "My people have committed two sins:**
> **They have forsaken me,**
> **the spring of living water,**
> **and have dug their own cisterns,**
> **broken cisterns that cannot hold water." (Jeremiah 2:13)**

5. How is self-protection like lighting one's own fire? Like digging one's own well?

6. God speaks pretty bluntly in these passages. How do you feel about a God who talks like this to you?

FAMILY GROUP

Meet together to read this section and discuss the questions. (20 minutes)

Failure of Self-Protection

Unfortunately, our wrong dependencies don't "work." They don't get us what we long for and were created to enjoy. We want to be accepted for who we are, but our self-protective masks and false dependencies keep us from even knowing who we are. We desire freedom to be authentic and carefree, but we end up bound to others' expectations of who we should be, expectations we ourselves helped to create. Living a lie, being someone we're really not, running desperately from our pain—that kind of "life" never deeply satisfies. However attractive the polished exterior of our lives, we never stop longing for someone to open the door of our prison and simply love the disheveled, imperfect inmate of our soul the way a mother embraces her play-soiled child.

And from behind the bars of our self-protective layers we can't offer freedom to anyone else either. If we free them to be themselves, they might let us down. If we love them for who they are, they might not change into who we need them to be for our benefit. Instead of loving others, we're committed to obligating them to love us. Our determination is not to give but to get, and the bondage becomes worse as the years pass.

7. Share with the group one of your dominant codependent strategies for self-protection and tell how it does or does not "work" to get you what you deeply want.

8.   a. If you were to abandon that strategy, what good would likely come of it?

     b. What bad would likely come of it?

9. What do you think would happen to your relationship with God in that circumstance?

FAMILY GROUP

Sinfulness of Self-Protection

What is so dangerous about our self-protection is that it seems so justified. We think we deserve our masks because we've been hurt so badly, and we consider God an ogre for demanding that we trust Him alone. We'd rather work at staying safe—safe from being hurt, safe from loving others in the "real world," safe from being alone with God. Our masks aren't just *unhelpful* because they don't get us what we want; they're wrong because they sabotage dependence on God. However well they may have worked to help us survive childhood losses, our adult codependent strategies run counter to our deepest obligations: trusting God and loving others.

The suggestion that our codependency is more an evidence of our fallenness than our woundedness may elicit outrage even for codependents committed to recovery. Does God really hold us culpable for our *reasonable* self-protective strategies? We've been wounded and *God allowed it*. What does it mean for a wounded heart to trust God?

The question demands more than a glib answer. Sorting out the pain we've experienced from the wrong we've done is difficult at best. But we must grapple with these deep questions of the heart, taking into account both God's compassion for our sorrow and His unflinching call for our faith and obedience. As His redeemed children we're told to trust Him with our very lives, and we must admit that codependency undermines our attempts to do so.

When we construct false selves in order to stay safe, we spurn the gospel of grace in favor of maintaining our independence from God. At the heart of codependent living is an arrogant and fear-based refusal to rely solely on God, an unwillingness to rest in His mercy, to be satisfied with His provision, and to set our hearts on obedience. Codependency is not just unhelpful, but dreadfully and crucially wrong.

Read John 6:28-29.

> **Then they asked him [Jesus], "What must we do to do the works God requires?"**
> **Jesus answered, "The work of God is this: to believe in the one he has sent."**

10. Jesus says that belief or trust in Him—not performing pious acts—is the main way we are to obey God. Why is it harder to believe than to do something for God?

11. a. Fear often keeps us from trusting Christ in a painful or difficult circumstance. Name some of your greatest fears.

b. Read Mark 5:35-36. Are faith and fear ever compatible? Why, or why not?

While Jesus was still speaking, some men came from the house of Jairus, the synagogue ruler. "Your daughter is dead," they said. "Why bother the teacher any more?"

Ignoring what they said, Jesus told the synagogue ruler, "Don't be afraid; just believe."

c. Jesus says, "Don't be afraid; just believe." What does that mean, and how do you do it?

d. What makes it easy or hard for you to believe instead of fearing?

FAMILY GROUP

Prayer Requests
(10 minutes)

Share your prayer requests with other family members. Volunteer to pray specifically for one other person during the coming week.

My prayer request is _____

_____

and _____ is praying for me.

I am praying for _____ and his/her prayer request is _____

_____

_____.

LARGE GROUP

A Word of Hope

(10 minutes)

When we begin to see the underlying sin of our self-protective codependency, we as believers have three choices: We can deny or justify our sinfulness; or we can despair of ever being loved by God; or we can confess and be forgiven because of Jesus' atonement. The Apostle John tells us:

> **If we claim to be without sin, we deceive ourselves and the truth is not in us. If we confess our sins, he is faithful and just and will forgive us our sins and purify us from all unrighteousness. (1 John 1:8-9)**

Prayer

Those who wish may repeat the Lord's Prayer.

During the Week

Write in your journal your favorite strategies for staying out of pain and safe from others (eating, working, shopping, nagging, rescuing, etc.). Compose a prayer of confession for those strategies, asking God to cleanse you not only from guilt, but also from the desire to pursue them rather than trust Him.

For more information on this week's topic, see *From Bondage to Bonding*, chapter 9. For more information regarding next week's topic, read chapter 11.

Benediction

Hear with your heart these words from Hebrews 13:20:

> **May the God of peace, who through the blood of the eternal covenant brought back from the dead our Lord Jesus, that great Shepherd of the sheep, equip you with everything good for doing his will, and may he work in us what is pleasing to him, through Jesus Christ, to whom be glory for ever and ever. Amen.**

Thinking God's Thoughts

Theme for meditation: GOD INVITES OUR TRUST.

Reading: Genesis 13:1-6
              Jeremiah 7:1-8
              Psalm 56:1-13
              Proverbs 29:25
              John 14:1-7
              Romans 9:30-33

Prayer:
    God, thank You for this evidence in Your Word that You invite our trust:
    God, thank You for these areas in my life where my trust in You has
         been rewarded:
    God, this is what I will do (or stop doing) to trust You in the coming week:

REPENTING OF OUR SIN

LARGE GROUP

This session will deal with grieving, though with a different slant than the grieving we explored in session 6. Keep in mind that our purpose in dealing with grief is not to become depressed but to find a deeper joy of living daily in God's grace. Encourage your fellow journeyers by saying a silent prayer right now for their healing (and your own).

Warm-up
(5 minutes)
1. Share with someone else an experience of victory you've had over one codependent trait during the last month.

ON YOUR OWN

> Read this section individually and complete the exercises that follow.
> (20 minutes)

Repenting of Our Layers

If we're to heal deeply and embrace a godly alternative to codependency, we must grieve our wrong layers of pretense and self-protection as well as grieving the pain of our losses. The grief is not the same.

Children resort to pretense in order to survive. In response to specific experiences of abuse or neglect and according to their individual temperaments, they adopt false selves to stay safe instead of learning to pursue other-centered love. As adults, those same children cling to their destructive self-protective strategies, and the wounded become the wounders.

Our past woundedness, however, is no excuse for our present layers. Childhood damage doesn't justify self-protective love failures. Even if we'd had perfect parents, we'd have struggled to remain independent from God and safe from other people. No one escapes the effect of the Fall. We're all flawed lovers, and it's not just our parents' fault. Our false selves do great harm to ourselves and others; we must face and grieve the damage. Scripture calls that kind of grief *repentance.*

Codependent strategies intended to protect us actually result in greater self-harm. Allowing ourselves to be controlled by others, for example, keeps us from the relationships we deeply desire. A marionette offers compliance, but compliance isn't intimacy. When we act like pawns in someone else's chess game, we destroy God's image in us. We must also repent of our self-contempt, our perverse denial of God's giftedness in us. When we neglect or hate or shame ourselves, when we withhold ourselves because we despise who we are, we call God a liar for affirming our preciousness (Isaiah 43:4) and refuse to bless those He's given us to love.

Our codependent layers also damage others. Our attempts to control others and our entrenched self-sufficiency are particularly harmful because no relationship can thrive in a control-based environment. We're built for freedom and mutual respect. Isolating ourselves and playing self-righteous games at church harm the Body of Christ. When we martyr ourselves to look good, we use others to stage our own melodrama, seeking applause at their expense. It's time for us to repent, becoming less preoccupied with how we feel or look and becoming willing to admit how we've damaged others. We must allow the full impact of our love failure to hit us as hard as if it had been done to us.

We hate admitting fault in a relationship where we've been accustomed to blaming the other person. We all want to believe we're only victims and not agents, but it's liberating to repent, asking for and receiving forgiveness for our wounding of God and others.

2. Write two things you've done this past week to damage yourself (for example, negative sentences you said to or about yourself, chosen re-victimization, negative words or actions you allowed others to use against you, etc.).

3. Next, write what it would look like to repent of that sin against yourself.

4. Think of one specific strategy you often use on someone close to you that protects you from genuinely engaging your true self on that person's behalf (for example, working long hours to avoid family demands, or using criticism instead of either empathy or discipline toward your children, or shopping sprees to avoid marital pain).

5. Write a note of confession to the person you've harmed, focusing on your sin, not the other person's sin.

Pray about whether or not to deliver the note

FAMILY GROUP

> Read this section aloud together and complete the exercises that follow.
> (30 minutes)

Repenting of Our Rebellion

What undergirds all of our codependent strategies is an avid commitment to making life work without God. Our autonomy offers us a way to protect ourselves without God's help; our niceness, helpfulness, or religiosity act as our "saviors." Wonderful as we may look on the outside, inside we raise quiet fists in defiance against God.

Our refusal to need God grieves Him. We think it's reasonable to light our own path in the emotional blackness caused by past and present losses, but God invites us to trust Him in the dark because He knows our greatest good is in trusting Him alone for the resources we need to live rich and meaningful lives. If "life" for us is intimate communion with a God who loves us, repentance and recovery will be difficult but joyfully possible. If, on the other hand, life is found in having, or trying to get, the intimacy and impact we want when and how we want it, we spit on the Cross and trample the gospel underfoot. We, the abused, become abusers of the One who died for us.

We must grieve not only about how bad things were (and are) for us but also about how wonderful we mistakenly thought we were all along. We must enter the Father's pain over the misery we bring on ourselves because of our autonomous independence from Him. When the Israelites repented after God had punished them for their idolatry, God finally "could bear Israel's misery no longer" (Judges 10:16). The image of God grieving over His people's deserved unhappiness is wondrous. Does He weep when we use the gifts He gives us to protect ourselves instead of bless others? Does He groan when we insist on trusting ourselves and not Him? Does He hurt when we do damage to ourselves by permitting abuse? We know very little of the wounded heart of God on our behalf.

Yet the Father's heart, though wounded, longs for restoration with His precious children, and it's our repentance that opens us to forgiveness and grace. God never turns from a repentant heart. David declared, "A broken and contrite heart, O God, you will not despise" (Psalm 51:17). Until we have acknowledged and repented of our sin and have tasted God's forgiveness, we can't forgive anyone else wholeheartedly.

6. What are some "respectable" (even religious) and some not-so-respectable things we might do to keep ourselves in charge of our own lives instead of depending utterly on God?

7. Name one thing you do to make life work without depending on God.

8. What might happen (bad and good) if you repent and quit doing that thing?

Read Isaiah 30:15-17.

> **This is what the Sovereign LORD, the Holy One of Israel, says:**
> **"In repentance and rest is your salvation,**
> **in quietness and trust is your strength,**
> **but you would have none of it.**
> **You said, 'No, we will flee on horses.'**

> **Therefore you will flee!**
> **You said, 'We will ride off on swift horses.'**
> **Therefore your pursuers will be swift!**
> **A thousand will flee**
> **at the threat of one;**
> **at the threat of five**
> **you will all flee away,**
> **till you are left**
> **like a flagstaff on a mountaintop,**
> **like a banner on a hill."**

9. a. According to Isaiah, what happens when we *refuse* to repent?

    b. How do you feel about what God says in this passage?

Read Luke 15:8-10.

> **[Jesus said,] "Suppose a woman has ten silver coins and loses one. Does she not light a lamp, sweep the house and search carefully until she finds it? And when she finds it, she calls her friends and neighbors together and says, 'Rejoice with me; I have found my lost coin.' In the same way, I tell you, there is rejoicing in the presence of the angels of God over one sinner who repents."**

10. How does God view our repentance?

FAMILY GROUP

> Remain together for the next section.
> (10 minutes)

How Should We Repent?

We must learn to weep over our sin. Perhaps the best way to enter repentance for our pretense and autonomy is to open our hearts to God's Word to us. Conviction of sin is a function of grace, a work the Holy Spirit does within us. He is relentless, even brutal, in carrying out His task of exposing our sin. Sometimes He works directly through a passage of Scripture or through His own quiet witness to our hearts as we "tune in" to the underlying dynamics of a given interaction with a friend or relative. At other times He uses the rebuke of a friend (or even an opponent) to open our eyes to our love failures. Solomon tells us in Proverbs 27:6, "Wounds from a friend can be trusted"; they usher us into conviction and godly sorrow. And as we walk through repentance into grace, the precious knowledge that we're loved as we are and that God's grace is sufficient makes us bold even to welcome reproof from God and others. "Where sin increased, grace increased all the more," said the Apostle Paul (Romans 5:20). Thanks be to God!

11. The apostles teach us that it is God's kindness that lead us to recognition of our sin and repentance. How have you experienced God's kindness in helping you recognize your failures to love?

> **Do you show contempt for the riches of his [God's] kindness, tolerance and patience, not realizing that God's kindness leads you toward repentance? (Romans 2:4)**

> **The Lord is not slow in keeping his promise, as some understand slowness. He is patient with you, not wanting anyone to perish, but everyone to come to repentance. (2 Peter 3:9)**

FAMILY GROUP

Prayer Requests
(10 minutes)
Share your prayer requests with other family members. Volunteer to pray specifically for one other person during the coming week.

My prayer request is _____

_____

and _____ is praying for me.

I am praying for _____ and his/her prayer request is _____

_____

_____.

LARGE GROUP

A Word of Hope
(10 minutes)
Listen again to Isaiah's encouraging words about facing and confessing our sin:

"In repentance and rest is your salvation, in quietness and trust is your strength." (Isaiah 30:15)

We can face our sin with courage because our confession draws us into the grace of forgiveness God offers through faith in Jesus. Praise His name!

Prayer
Those who wish may join in repeating the Lord's Prayer, especially focusing on the petition for forgiveness.

During the Week
Write a statement in your journal covenanting with God to be open this week to His exposure of sin in your life. Keep a record of what He shows you and what you do about it.

For more information on this week's topic, see *From Bondage to Bonding*, chapter 11. For more information regarding next week's topic, read chapter 12.

Benediction
Hear the ancient priestly blessing:

> **The LORD bless you**
>   **and keep you;**
> **the LORD make his face shine upon you**
>   **and be gracious to you;**
> **the LORD turn his face toward you**
>   **and give you peace. (Numbers 6:24)**

Thinking God's Thoughts
Theme for meditation: GOD FORGIVES THE REPENTANT.

Reading: Exodus 34:1-10
                Jeremiah 31:18-20
                Psalm 51:14-19
                Hosea 14:1-4
                Mark 1:1-8
                2 Corinthians 7:8-11

Prayer:
    Lord, thank You for this evidence in Your Word that You forgive the repentant:
    Lord, thank You for these areas in my life where You've forgiven me when
        I've repented:
    Lord, this is how I will show my repentance for my layers (against others) and
        my rebellion (against You):

GRACE FOR THE CONTRITE

Welcome. Whether this has been a terrific week, a terrible week, or something in between, remember that God loves you and is working out His eternal purposes in your life, even when you're not consciously aware of His movement.

Warm-up
(5 minutes)
1. Find someone from your family group and tell each other one way your relationship with God is different from what it was one year ago.

> Read this section to yourself and write answers to the questions that follow.
> (10 minutes)

Admitting Our Helplessness
Grieving our losses and repenting of our self-protection are essential to recovery from codependency, but owning our woundedness and recognizing our self-protection doesn't go far enough. What we need is a solution to our dilemma of pain and guilt.

In our attempt to satisfy our deepest desires, we have attached them to behaviors, things, or people we think can satisfy our thirst for connectedness, acceptance, freedom, and forgiveness—what we ultimately desire primarily from God. These attachments (to a substance, an idea, a spouse, a job, etc.) are compulsive but ultimately disillusioning. We are kidnapped by our false attachments, imprisoned by our codependency, and unable to liberate ourselves.

The first step in the Alcoholics Anonymous (AA) recovery program says, *"We admitted we were powerless over alcohol—that our lives had become unmanageable."* In other words, the alcoholic admitted his addiction was so compulsive as to prevent his will from controlling it; his attachment to alcohol ultimately superseded his every attempt to "straighten up." And no power can be available to quit the habit until that first step is taken: the admission of powerlessness.

For some codependents, the first step might mean acknowledging helplessness over drugs or alcohol—dealing with their own addiction before dealing with the codependency undergirding it. Substance abuse and codependency often go hand in hand. But even nonaddicted codependents must take the first step in recovery, admitting they are powerless over the person or relational habit to which they've attached their desires. Acknowledging our inability to manage our lives is excruciating but altogether necessary.

2. What kinds of things have you said or done to keep from admitting your addiction (to a substance, a habit, a person, etc.)?

3. What is the effect on your close relationships when you refuse to admit your helplessness and try instead to control people (including yourself) and circumstances?

4. Do you feel ready to take Step One, to acknowledge your powerlessness over your false attachments? If so, write a "Step One" sentence acknowledging one area of powerlessness in your life.

Share your answers to questions 2 through 4.
(15 minutes)
Remain together to read this section and to complete the exercises that follow.
(25 minutes)

Asking God for Help

When we come to the end of ourselves (which is God's purpose for us all) we realize that help must come from beyond ourselves. AA's Step Two says, *"We came to believe that a Power greater than ourselves could restore us to sanity."* When we face the limits of our humanness by admitting our powerlessness, we're ready for God's grace. In fact, it is in our very inability to perfect ourselves that our hope appears, because in our helplessness we are forced to recognize that we stand in desperate need of God.

King David is described as "a man after [God's] own heart" (1 Samuel 13:14). As a shepherd boy, he learned utter dependence on God's help during many years of sheeptending and later while being murderously pursued by King Saul (1 Samuel 18–27). Eventually, God allowed King Saul to be defeated, gave David victory over all his enemies, and established David as king over all Israel. Unfortunately, after several years of godly rule, David took back from God control over his own life and engaged in a premeditated adulterous affair with Bathsheba the wife of Uriah, one of David's generals. David then plotted to have Uriah killed in order to cover up his guilt.

God's prophet Nathan confronted David with his sin, and David had to turn to God for help of a different kind: help in dealing with his sin. His autonomy from God and his adultery/murder against his subjects had to be confronted and repented.

We, too, must face more than just the woundedness of our past and our helplessness to control the people and circumstances in our lives. We must face the realization that we are determined to be independent of God and to run our lives our own way, hurting other people in the process. The help we need is not just for God's strength in the face of our weakness, but for His forgiveness in the face of our sin.

When David repented of his crime against Bathsheba and Uriah, he wrote a prayer of confession: Psalm 51.

Have mercy on me, O God,
**   according to your unfailing love;**
according to your great compassion
**   blot out my transgressions.**
Wash away all my iniquity
**   and cleanse me from my sin.**
**   (Psalm 51:1-2)**

Read aloud the verses on the following pages from Psalm 51, and discuss with your family group the questions in between.

5. In verses 1-2, David asks for mercy, compassion, and cleansing. Do you identify with those desires? Explain.

> **For I know my transgressions,**
>   **and my sin is ever before me.**
> **Against you, you only, have I sinned**
>   **and done what is evil in your sight,**
> **so that you are proved right when you speak**
>   **and justified when you judge. (Psalm 51:3-4)**

6. David says he has sinned "only" against God, even though he has clearly harmed both Bathsheba and Uriah. What do you think he means? What does this teach us about the true nature of our own codependent strategies?

> **Cleanse me with hyssop, and I will be clean;**
>   **wash me, and I will be whiter than snow.**
> **Let me hear joy and gladness;**
>   **let the bones you have crushed rejoice.**
> **Hide your face from my sins**
>   **and blot out all my iniquity. (Psalm 51:7-9)**

7. David applies to his situation the ritual God had instituted by which the priests would dip a branch of hyssop in blood or water to sprinkle (and thereby "clean") anyone who was ceremonially unclean. The shed blood of Jesus on the cross ties into this image for us as repentant believers.

Do you ever feel dirty because of things you've done? How easy is it for you to believe that God can make you clean?

> **Create in me a pure heart, O God,**
>   **and renew a steadfast spirit within me.**
> **Do not cast me from your presence**
>   **or take your Holy Spirit from me.**
> **Restore to me the joy of your salvation**
>   **and grant me a willing spirit, to sustain me.**
>
> **Then I will teach transgressors your ways,**
>   **and sinners will turn back to you.**
> **Save me from bloodguilt, O God,**
>   **the God who saves me,**
>   **and my tongue will sing of your righteousness.**

**O Lord, open my lips,
and my mouth will declare your praise. (Psalm 51:10-15)**

8. David asked forgiveness not just for his own sake but so that he could bless the lives of others. How might this prayer be lived out in your relationships?

FAMILY GROUP

Remain together to read the next section and discuss the questions that follow.
(15 minutes)

Empowering Grace

Through the words of the prophet Nathan, God offered David forgiveness when he acknowledged and repented of his sin:

**Then David said to Nathan, "I have sinned against the LORD."
Nathan replied, "The LORD has taken away your sin. You are not going to die." (2 Samuel 12:13)**

God offers the same forgiving grace to us when we repent.

But there is also another kind of grace available to us as recovering codependents: *empowering grace* for our self-protective layers. God offers us love beyond our own ability for the unlovable people in our lives. He provides the power to behave in a way consistent with others' good, even when we're deeply hurt ourselves. For recovering codependents this is an essential grace; our strategies for escaping pain in ways that protect us but damage others are impossible to change through our own willpower.

As we spend time quieting ourselves in God's presence to hear Him speak His love to us, His grace changes us, sometimes dramatically, sometimes imperceptibly. When we repent of our self-protective strategies and receive God's grace to cover our sin, we are transformed by the transaction. In repentance we sink our roots deep into the fertile ground of grace, and the fruit of God's Spirit buds and matures without our striving or straining. It's only when we refuse grace and try to live and love apart from God that we wither and die. To love without our layers we must live connected to Him.

9. How easy is it for you to quiet yourself to hear the Holy Spirit tell you God loves you? Why is that?

10. a. What discourages you from believing that the power to change is really available?

b. What encourages you to believe that?

Prayer Requests

(10 minutes)
Share your prayer requests with other family members. Volunteer to pray specifically for one other person during the coming week.

My prayer request is _____

_____

and _____ is praying for me.

I am praying for _____ and his/her prayer request is _____

_____

_____.

A Word of Hope

(10 minutes)
David declared that God will surely hear our confession and forgive us when our hearts are broken because we see our sin:

> **The sacrifices of God are a broken spirit;**
> **a broken and contrite heart,**
> **O God, you will not despise. (Psalm 51:17)**

Prayer

All who wish may join in repeating the Serenity Prayer.

During the Week

Memorizing Scripture can be simply a ritual, but it can also be a way to store important truths in our hearts. First John 1:8-9 offers us continual assurance of forgiveness in the presence of confessed sin. You may wish to begin memorizing it this week.

If we claim to be without sin, we deceive ourselves and the truth is not in us. If we confess our sins, he is faithful and just and will forgive us our sins and purify us from all unrighteousness. (1 John 1:8-9)

Also, spend some time alone in God's presence. If you have trouble quieting your churning brain, try writing in your journal about your struggle to be with Him. Ask Him to teach you how to listen to Him.

For more information on this week's topic, see *From Bondage to Bonding,* chapter 12. For more information regarding next week's topic, read chapter 5.

Benediction

Hear the words of the Apostle Paul:

May the grace of the Lord Jesus Christ, and the love of God, and the fellowship of the Holy Spirit be with you all. (2 Corinthians 13:14)

Thinking God's Thoughts

Theme for meditation: GOD OFFERS GRACE TO THE CONTRITE.

Reading: Nehemiah 9:1-6,16-21
                  Isaiah 30:15-18
                  Psalm 130:1-8
                  Proverbs 3:33-35
                  John 1:1-5,14-18
                  Ephesians 2:1-10

Prayer:
      God, thank You for this evidence in Your Word that You offer grace
            to the contrite:
      God, thank You for these areas in my life where You've shown
            Your forgiving grace to me:
      God, this is what I will do (or stop doing) to look to You alone for grace:

PART THREE

ANTIDEPENDENCE

DETERMINED TO STAY SAFE

Welcome again! As you're becoming more familiar with what codependency looks like, are you also checking out how closely your own style of relating fits the description? Don't be discouraged if you're finding you're more codependent than you thought. God offers not just recognition of our flaws but also hope for forgiveness and change. Persevere!

Warm-up

(5 minutes)

1. Turn to someone near you and tell each other what it's been like as you've tried to lay hold of grace this week.

> Read this section together, then discuss the questions that follow.
> (30 minutes)

Refusal to Risk or Trust

An earlier session focused on the codependent characteristic of low self-esteem, common to people from addictive or abusive homes. But the flip side of self-contempt is also common to codependents: a self-sufficiency that says, "I'll run my own life and do things my way. Asking for help is a sign of weakness, and I refuse to appear weak."

We codependents typically refuse to need or trust others. Self-sufficiency for some of us was necessary for survival because of our childhood abuse or abandonment. The little child who was seven going on twenty-three may have had to be that way to keep the family from falling apart. Neediness can also be shameful, especially for those of us humiliated as children for having had normal childhood anger, fear, or sadness. The refusal to need or trust sometimes seemed absolutely imperative.

Alongside our unspoken refusal to need is our fearful refusal to take risks in relationships. It's scary to offer who we are to another human being. We might be

119

scorned, rejected, ignored, or (worst of all perhaps) abused. Of course we can't genuinely love someone without offering ourselves, so we're caught in a no-win dilemma: Risk loving and most likely be hurt, or withhold ourselves and stay safe but lonely.

Taking risks is the doorway to freedom, but it feels like the doorway to death for codependents. Driven by a compulsion to never rock the boat, we are terrified of being spontaneous, carefree, or wrong. We're not free ourselves, nor can we offer freedom to others. Rather than risk change and healing, we will rigidly cling to the predictable and depend only on ourselves, even if it's painful and destructive.

2. Do you identify with this section? What are some statements that sound especially like you?

3. What experiences in your past make it hard for you to need or trust others?

4. What signs of fearing to need or trust others do you see in yourself these days?

5. In these two passages, how does Jesus depend on others and lay Himself open to being disappointed by people?

> **Jesus traveled about from one town and village to another, proclaiming the good news of the kingdom of God. The Twelve were with him, and also some women who had been cured of evil spirits and diseases: Mary (called Magdalene) from whom seven demons had come out; Joanna the wife of Cuza, the manager of Herod's household; Susanna; and many others. These women were helping to support them out of their own means. (Luke 8:1-3)**

> **Jesus went with his disciples to a place called Gethsemane, and he said to them, "Sit here while I go over there and pray." He took Peter and the two sons of Zebedee along with him, and he began to be sorrowful and troubled. Then he said to them, "My soul is overwhelmed with sorrow to the point of death. Stay here and keep watch with me."**
> 　　**Going a little farther, he fell with his face to the ground and prayed, "My Father, if it is possible, may this cup be taken from me. Yet not as I will, but as you will."**

**Then he returned to his disciples and found them sleeping.
"Could you men not keep watch with me for one hour?" he asked
Peter. "Watch and pray so that you will not fall into temptation.
The spirit is willing, but the body is weak." (Matthew 36:36-41)**

6. Jesus' friends slept while He struggled, then ran away and pretended not to know Him. But He was able to open His heart to them after this betrayal. Does God ask us to do the same? How do you feel about that?

ON YOUR OWN

> Read this section to yourself, then answer the questions that follow.
> (15 minutes)

Perfectionism

Another evidence of self-sufficiency is the belief that we must be perfect in order to be approved—by ourselves or anyone else. We drive ourselves crazy trying to figure out what the important people in our lives expect from us at any given moment so we can react perfectly. As often as not, we guess wrong and end up "imperfect" despite our best intentions. To make matters worse, we usually feel compelled to please everyone we meet, so we train ourselves to be "psychic" in order never to disappoint anyone.

In the end, however, our perfectionism is nothing but a facade, an attempt to make life well-ordered and attractive on the outside, even though everything is messy and out of control on the inside. The externally "perfect" life is an illusion, a false image of "togetherness" we desperately want to believe and want others to believe in order to avoid the pain of what things are really like.

More than that, we perfectionists are out to prove that who we are is beyond reproach, beyond criticism, and untouchable. Perfectionism is an angry, prideful attempt never to have to ask forgiveness or owe anything to anyone, including God. We say, in effect, "I will come out looking good no matter what the cost to me or anyone else. *No one* can fault me, not even God; *everyone* will have to admire me." Perfectionism is the antithesis of grace.

A common (often unconscious) misunderstanding of the Bible is that we are *saved* because of God's love (not our good deeds), but after that we have to maintain God's approval by working really hard. The Apostle Paul addressed that misconception when he wrote to the Galatian believers:

> **You foolish Galatians! Who has bewitched you? Before your very
> eyes Jesus Christ was clearly portrayed as crucified. I would like to
> learn just one thing from you: Did you receive the Spirit by
> observing the law, or by believing what you heard? Are you so
> foolish? After beginning with the Spirit, are you now trying to
> attain your goal by human effort? Have you suffered so much for**

nothing—if it really was for nothing? Does God give you his Spirit and work miracles among you because you observe the law, or because you believe what you heard? (Galatians 3:1-5)

Our Christian life is meant to be lived by grace, not by trying to be perfect. God isn't shocked when we fail to live up to our standards of perfection. He isn't even surprised (saddened, certainly, but not surprised) when we do something wrong deliberately. Jesus died because God knew we were hopelessly corrupt without help. The Crucifixion was God's way of saying, "I know how bad you are, and you're in fact worse than you think." It was also His reassurance: "I know the worst about you, and it's forgiven."

7. Do you feel compelled to be perfect? Why do you suppose you feel that way? In other words, what would you gain if you *could* be perfect?

8. How does your perfectionism work against your trust in God? Try to be specific.

FAMILY GROUP

Take turns reading this section and discuss the ques-
tions that follow.
(20 minutes)

Isolation

Another aspect of the codependent's self-sufficiency is isolation, the tendency to shun others who might see what's going on and challenge it. We codependents are often bound to an unspoken code of secrecy about our personal and family dysfunction. No one but Jenny's closest sister, for example, knew about Brad's drinking. Sexual abuse victims usually don't talk, either. The loyalty imperative in an abusive family is incredibly strong. Often the shame is so great *no one* in the family will deal with the problem, let alone talk to anyone else about it. Isolation includes not just secrecy, but also avoiding involvement with anyone who might discover the secret if they got close enough.

Isolation is also a control issue. To let others in behind the carefully maintained propriety would be to admit things are out of control, that we are unable to manage our lives effectively. Thus we become experts at isolation as a strategy for looking good and for supporting the illusion of normalcy. It may be excruciatingly lonely, but it's preferable to facing the shame.

9. Name some ways you manage to stay isolated.

10. How do the following affect your relationship with God?

- Unwillingness to trust

- Perfectionism

- Isolation and self-trust

11. Break the code of secrecy by telling each other one good thing and one bad thing about your childhood family life.

FAMILY GROUP

Prayer Requests
(10 minutes)
Share your prayer requests with other family members. Volunteer to pray specifically for one other person during the coming week.

My prayer request is _____

_____

and _____ is praying for me.

I am praying for _____ and his/her prayer request is _____

_____

_____ .

A Word of Hope
(10 minutes)
Paul assured the congregation of believers in Rome (and us, as well) that they would know joy, peace, and realistic hope if, and only if, they would risk putting their trust in God, not themselves. He writes,

> **May the God of hope fill you with all joy and peace as you trust in him, so that you may overflow with hope by the power of the Holy Spirit. (Romans 15:13)**

Prayer
All who wish may repeat the Serenity Prayer together.

During the Week
Write a paragraph about the good things you remember from your growing-up years in your family of origin. Write another paragraph about the bad things. Then check with someone who knew you back then (like a sibling or aunt) and ask that person to honestly assess your memories. Are they accurate? Happier than things really were? Worse than things really were?

For more information on this week's topic, see *From Bondage to Bonding*, chapter 5. For more information regarding the topic of next week's session, read chapter 10.

Benediction
Hear the words of God through the Apostle Peter:

> **Grow in the grace and knowledge of our Lord and Savior Jesus Christ. To him be glory both now and forever! Amen. (2 Peter 3:18)**

Thinking God's Thoughts
Theme for meditation: GOD IS TRUSTWORTHY.

Reading: Exodus 14:5-28
                    2 Chronicles 20:1-26
                    Psalm 103:1-6
                    Proverbs 28:26
                    Matthew 11:25-30
                    Romans 4:1-8

Prayer:

Lord, thank You for this evidence in Your Word of how trustworthy You are:

Lord, thank You for these areas in my life where You've shown Yourself trustworthy to me:

Lord, this is what I will do (or stop doing) to evidence my willingness to trust You and not myself:

ANGER TOWARD OTHERS

This group has hopefully become like a family to you, a place where you can be heard without condemnation, a place where people love and accept you in Jesus' name and on His behalf. Though it's still risky to disclose who you really are, even to this group, be encouraged to know your risk-taking pleases the Father, who wants you to experience mutual interdependence within this fellowship of the redeemed. Keep growing!

Warm-up
(5 minutes)

1. Join with a partner and share with each other what you learned during the week as you "checked out" your perceptions of what life was like in your family of origin.

Anger

One emotion almost always repressed among adult codependents is intense anger—rage, really—over their childhood and present losses. Even when the damage is unintentional—as in the case of a parent's death or a

> In your family group, take a poll to see whether everyone's memories were happier, sadder, or mostly accurate in comparison with how things really were. Then read this section aloud and discuss the questions that follow.
> (25 minutes)

loved one's unavoidable absence—the losses inevitably cause deep anger. As children we may have been forbidden or unable to verbalize our rage, and even as adults we may be unaware of it. We may, in fact, have disguised our anger as a biting sense of humor, or we may have misdirected it by dumping it on someone or something other than where it really belongs.

Our anger—though camouflaged or displaced—is still there if it hasn't been processed. When anger is admitted and felt, over time it will disappear. But if it isn't felt, it stays, just waiting to be felt. Unacknowledged anger goes underground, not away.

2. Does depending on no one but yourself seem like an attractive option for you? Why, or why not?

3. Are you aware of anger in yourself against God or people? If so, what are you angry about?

4. Which is harder for you: to let yourself feel your anger or to control the anger you feel?

5. In what ways (besides saying how you feel) do you generally communicate your anger toward others?

ON YOUR OWN

> Read this section to yourself and answer the questions that follow.
> (15 minutes)

Autonomy

Sometimes our anger surfaces as an assertion of antidependence in relationship to others. This autonomy, in fact, masquerades as "health" for some recovering code-pendents, who believe "getting in touch" with their anger grants them permission to disassociate permanently from anyone who has hurt or is hurting them. This self-sufficient "solution," however, actually undergirds rather than heals the codependency.

Contemporary culture is intoxicated with the heady wine of independence. We sing songs, wage verbal battles, and argue court cases over the notion of personal autonomy and individual "rights." We're told to become independent—politically, financially, ethically, religiously, and relationally. "Do your own thing." "Be your own person." "Become self-actualized." "Demand your rights." "Look out for Number One."

Personal autonomy implies that a person can get along just fine without depending on God and/or other people. Many recovering codependents are determined to make it on their own, to stay in control, or to regain control over their own lives without having to ask for help. Having been badly damaged, they've decided, "Never again. I'll only enter relationships where I'm in charge. I'll generate my own acceptance, forgiveness, and empowerment." The assumption is that we're the only ones who can truly love and provide for ourselves, so it's absurd to depend on anyone else.

While it is surely foolish to believe someone exists who will love us without ever disappointing us, nevertheless we must admit we can't depend on our *own* opinion of ourselves, either. We don't always like ourselves, often with good reason. We can't always forgive ourselves, we're not always lovable, and our own self-esteem is fickle, at best. On the other hand, we also tend to view ourselves as better than we really are, justifying our flaws and ignoring our deep failure to love. We need something beyond other people's opinion of us, and beyond our own opinion of ourselves, to use as a reference point for our self-acceptance.

What we need is Someone who will never waver in His valuing of us or in His commitment to our well-being, Someone whose forgiveness and empowerment is utterly reliable. No one will do but God Himself.

We cannot manufacture our own acceptance, but we can find it in God. A reasonable alternative to either other-based approval or self-generated acceptance is to define our worth based on how God sees us. We cannot meet our own needs, regardless of our anger at how others have let us down. Vengeful antidependence toward others may harden us to feeling our pain, but it will leave us ambiguous about our value and deeply lonely.

6. Which of these three choices best describes the way you usually decide how to view yourself? Explain.

- Based on what other people think of me

- Based on my own opinions of myself

- Based on what God thinks of me

7. How has that been good or bad for you?

8. Read these passages, then write why God thinks we are arrogant if we look to ourselves for acceptance, forgiveness, and empowerment.

> **Do not be wise in your own eyes;**
> **fear the LORD and shun evil. (Proverbs 3:7)**

> **Now listen, you who say, "Today or tomorrow we will go to this or that city, spend a year there, carry on business and make money." Why, you do not even know what will happen tomorrow. What is your life? You are a mist that appears for a little while and then vanishes. Instead, you ought to say, "If it is the Lord's will, we will live and do this or that." As it is, you boast and brag. All such boasting is evil. (James 4:13-16)**

9. What would you like to tell or ask God if He were standing next to you right now?

FAMILY GROUP

Take turns reading this section; then discuss the questions that follow.
(25 minutes)

Revenge and Demandingness

When our priority in relationships is self-protection from pain, we thwart God's purpose in those relationships: a freely chosen willingness to offer ourselves to others. Our angry withholding of ourselves and our determined intent to not need others keep us from the connectedness for which we naturally long. Too easily, recovering codependents rush to become independent of even committed relationships like marriage in order to find safety from being hurt again.

Autonomy blocks intimacy. Instead of enhancing closeness by alleviating demandingness, antidependence makes even more demands—that the other "be there" for us because we've discovered that's what we need and deserve. We codependents are essentially self-preoccupied even in recovery. In our hurry to "get well" we often neglect everyone else's needs or feelings, our process bulldozing forward at others' expense. We may drop our subtlety and just tell others how angry we are and how awful we think they are, dumping our rage in revenge for their neglect or mistreatment. If we stop at the point of getting in touch with and expressing our anger (and many do stop there), we won't ever "recover" according to God's design. Anger and demandingness are stops along the way, not our final destination.

When we simply vent our anger and reject our legitimate need for others, we violate our redeemed nature, which is to give and receive love from others out of the abundance of love God has shown us. Much as we might desire revenge—and much as the other person might deserve it—we *can* choose to experience our anger *without* pursuing vengeance (i.e., without making the other person somehow "pay"). God's directive to love is not canceled out by the failure of others to have loved us well. That directive—along with the command that we worship God above all else—is still the reason we're here on earth.

10. How has your anger at your losses kept you from loving others well?

11. How do you usually make people "pay" for hurting or rejecting you? (Others in the group may be able to tell what their experience of your "vengeance" has been, but don't ask unless you're sure you are ready to hear it.)

12. Paul instructed us not to let the sun go down while we are still angry (Ephesians 4:26). But it's not always possible to stop being angry quickly if we have nursed or repressed our anger. Do you think Paul means we have only one day to feel our anger? Explain.

13. Think about this: What should we do as Christians when we are angry at those who have harmed us? Take turns reading aloud these "steps" for handling anger, along with the accompanying Scripture passages.

Step 1: Admit the anger to yourself and God.

"In your anger do not sin": Do not let the sun go down while you are still angry. (Ephesians 4:26)

Step 2: Ask God's forgiveness for any "nursed" anger.

"But I tell you that anyone who is angry with his brother will be subject to judgment." (Matthew 5:22)

Step 3: Choose not to seek revenge.

Do not take revenge, my friends, but leave room for God's wrath, for it is written, "It is mine to avenge; I will repay," says the Lord. (Romans 12:19)

Step 4: Choose whether and how to verbalize your anger to anyone besides God, based on what is loving (i.e., good for) the other person.

Instead, speaking the truth in love, we will in all things grow up into him who is the Head, that is, Christ. (Ephesians 4:15)

14. What would you do if you tried all of these steps and were still angry?

Prayer Requests

(10 minutes)

Share your prayer requests with other family members. Volunteer to pray specifically for one other person during the coming week.

My prayer request is _____

_____

and _____ is praying for me.

I am praying for _____ and his/her prayer request is _____

_____

_____.

A Word of Hope

(10 minutes)

Anger is normal when we experience loss. Sometimes it reflects God's own anger against sin and injustice. God hears our anger and doesn't condemn us for it, though He forbids us to take revenge. Once we admit our anger to God, we're free to obey Jesus' words: "Love your enemies and pray for those who persecute you" (Matthew 5:44). That may be a long process and may require Christian counseling, but hope for dealing biblically with our anger is available to all believers.

Prayer

Those who wish may repeat the Lord's Prayer.

During the Week

Write in your journal whatever angry feelings surface this week toward people who harmed you (past or present). Write out the angry sentences you have in your head about them, perhaps in a letter you don't intend to send. Read the letter aloud to God. Then choose to pray for that person and decide whether, how, and when to express your anger.

For more information on this week's topic, see *From Bondage to Bonding,* chapter 10, which also covers next week's topic.

Benediction

Receive to your hearts these words from the writer of the book of Hebrews:

May the God of peace, who through the blood of the eternal covenant brought back from the dead our Lord Jesus, that great Shepherd of the sheep, equip you with everything good for doing his will, and may he work in us what is pleasing to him, through Jesus Christ, to whom be glory for ever and ever. Amen. (Hebrews 13:20)

Thinking God's Thoughts

Theme for meditation: GOD HEARS OUR ANGER.

Reading: Genesis 4:1-8
Jonah 4:1-11
Psalm 73:1-14
Proverbs 15:1
Mark 3:1-6
James 1:19-25

Prayer:
God, thank You for this evidence in Your Word that You know my anger:
God, thank You that You forgive these angry thoughts of revenge:
God, this is what I choose to do right now about the anger I don't really want to look at:

ANTIDEPENDENCE TOWARD GOD

Congratulations! You have invested over three months in this community process toward healing from codependency. The entire journey will be lifelong, of course, but you can take pride in having persevered this long. Keep up the good work!

Warm-up
(5 minutes)
1. Tell someone near you about a specific incident in the last few weeks that shows you're not as codependent now as you were three months ago.

> Individually, read this section
> and answer the questions.
> (15 minutes)

Antidependence: A Refusal of Grace
Though God is interested in having us face the pain of our unmet longings with integrity, He ultimately desires that we go beyond simply dealing with our woundedness. Our problem is much deeper than a poor self-image and an over-developed need for others' approval because we have not been loved well. A Twelve-Step program or some one-on-one counseling alone will not correct the destructive course on which we are bent. There are more serious heart issues that need to be addressed.

Our deepest problem is our arrogant rebellion—our chronic refusal to obey God—and our further refusal to repent and trust His grace. Deep in our hearts is a fist raised against God, a spirit of autonomy that says, "I'm a better judge of what's right in this situation than God is; I more than He deserve to call the shots." We worship at the shrine of our own self-sufficiency, and God judges our antidependence as worthy of the death penalty.

134

Can we deal with our codependency without acknowledging the rebellion and arrogance in our souls? Important as it is to face our woundedness, isn't our ultimate dilemma more related to our sin than our pain? Is not our deepest problem the fierce independence from God that undergirds our codependent strategies? Our fists are raised in God's face when we scramble to manage our lives apart from Him.

Our autonomy must be admitted and repented if we're to experience deep healing. Genuine life flows from our ongoing experience of connectedness to God as we receive and live in His grace. When we detach from Him and determine to follow our own agendas for making life work, we thwart grace and choke off God's life in us.

2. Do you have a fist raised in God's face? Do you identify with the attitude, "I'm a better judge of what's good for me in this situation than God is"? Explain.

3. If you said yes to question 2, name specific ways you act as though you think you know better than God.

4. If you said no, describe what it's like for you to yield to God's rule. Does anything make it hard for you to let God be in charge?

FAMILY GROUP

Read this section together and discuss the questions that follow.
(25 minutes)

Rage Against God

We recovering codependents are often unable or unwilling to lean wholly on God for His grace. We would rather find our strength in ourselves. Our spirit of antidependence can be defined as follows:

> Antidependence is a self-sufficient way of life in which a person attempts to generate his or her own acceptance, forgiveness, and empowerment apart from God. This results in spiritual rebellion, a distorted view of self, and problems with intimacy.

Whatever reasons we give for our entrenched autonomy, at the deepest levels of our souls our antidependence flows from our anger against God. We have expectations of what He should do (or should have done) for us, and we're enraged He isn't doing it (or didn't do it) in the way or at the time we thought was right. We may not even acknowledge the anger in our souls, but there are sure signs it is there nevertheless. It may take the form of nagging self-pity, a free-floating dissatisfaction with life and relationships, a quiet conviction that we deserve something better, an absence of genuine gratitude for God's gifts, or a lack of love for or inner connectedness with God. We may go so far as to wonder whether we even need or want grace. Our core of hardness and self-sufficiency, that inner stronghold of resistance to grace, grieves the Father, who designed us to love and trust Him.

Our recurring antidependence flows from our disappointment with God and our unwillingness to trust Him again. We'd rather depend on ourselves because in our hearts' dark corners we think we're more trustworthy than He. And in a way, we're right. We can't trust God to give us what we most want: a pain-free life in this world. His agenda (making us people who can love well and furthering the growth of His Kingdom) often conflicts with our agenda (avoiding pain). Turning from antidependence includes abandoning our deeply cherished agenda—deciding to care more about being people who love well than about escaping pain.

In our heads we know God is compassionate and loving because Scripture says so. But in our hearts we think that if He really loved us, He'd make the pain go away. Then, when we reject Him as unloving, we cut ourselves off from what we most long for: the kind of purely loving relationship that no human can supply. We're angry that God won't give us what we need even while we're refusing to receive it on His terms.

5. Tell about an incident in which God did not "come through" as you expected when you turned to Him.

6. How did you feel toward God then?

FAMILY GROUP

Continue with your family group for this section. (15 minutes)

The Case of Job

Job was in this situation: He was suffering terribly, not because he'd done something to deserve it, but for some reason he hadn't been told. Actually, God was letting Job suffer in order to prove to Satan and perhaps the other angels that He didn't need to buy Job's love with blessings. God wanted to prove that Job loved Him for who He was, not for what He did for Job. But God didn't bother to explain this reason to Job.

Job felt cheated. He had thought he and God were friends, but he considered this a lousy way to treat a friend. He demanded that God show up and defend His behavior. God responded because He liked the persistent way Job pursued their friendship and counted on God's faithfulness. But He didn't like Job's arrogance, so His response flattened Job's pride.

> The LORD spoke to Job out of the storm:
> **"Brace yourself like a man;**
> **I will question you,**
> **and you shall answer me.**
>
> **"Would you discredit my justice?**
> **Would you condemn me to justify yourself?**
> **Do you have an arm like God's,**
> **and can your voice thunder like his?**
> **Then adorn yourself with glory and splendor,**
> **and clothe yourself in honor and majesty.**
> **Unleash the fury of your wrath,**
> **look at every proud man and bring him low,**
> **look at every proud man and humble him,**
> **crush the wicked where they stand.**

> Bury them all in the dust together;
> shroud their faces in the grave." (Job 40:6-13)

Job's experience suggests that rejecting antidependence will require us to kill our pride (not just swallow it) and to persistently pursue friendship with a God who doesn't think He owes us any explanations for His actions.

7. What made the difference to Job was that God revealed His greatness to him. Job said,

> My ears had heard of you
> but now my eyes have seen you. (Job 42:5)

God revealed Himself because Job desired to meet with God more than anything else. Where does that leave you? What would it take for you to desire to meet God more than anything else, especially more than hanging on to your pride?

8. Job's conclusion after he had seen God was this:

> Therefore I despise myself
> and repent in dust and ashes. (Job 42:6)

a. How does Job's repentance fit into his experience with God?

b. How does your repentance fit into your experience with God?

ON YOUR OWN

Read this section to yourself and answer the questions that follow.
(10 minutes)

Abdicating Our Thrones

Though we might not say it quite this way, we are committed to staying on the throne of our own lives. We will not dethrone ourselves. We may acknowledge God's general sovereignty over His world, but we refuse it in our own hearts. There we intend to be king or queen, sovereign over our own world.

God is good, but we must also remember He is not to be trifled with. In C. S.

Lewis's book *The Lion, the Witch and the Wardrobe*, when the children discover that Aslan (the Christ figure) is a lion, this conversation with the Beavers follows:

> "Ooh!" said Susan, "I'd thought he was a man. Is he—quite safe? I shall feel rather nervous about meeting a lion."
>
> "That you will, dearie, and no mistake," said Mrs. Beaver, "if there's anyone who can appear before Aslan without their knees knocking, they're either braver than most or else just silly."
>
> "Then he isn't safe?" said Lucy.
>
> "Safe?" said Mr. Beaver. "Don't you hear what Mrs. Beaver tells you? Who said anything about safe? 'Course he isn't safe. But he's good. He's the king, I tell you."[1]

To God's enemies, to those who rebel against His just rule, He is a fierce and fearsome warrior. He demands our submission and our obedience, and we are wrong to think we can dethrone Him and enthrone ourselves with impunity.

If we refuse His grace, we refuse life. If we would be the god or goddess of our life, God can't be God and we jeopardize our relationship with Him. Today again He calls us to bow the knee and call Him God instead of shaking our rebellious fists in His face. Who will run your life, you or God? It is a question we face and answer daily, and we answer it not with words but with actions.

9. How would you feel about having your life run by an untamed lion of whom it can be said, "'Course he isn't safe. But he's good"? Why do you feel that way?

10. What can you do to let God be the God who rules your life?

FAMILY GROUP

Prayer Requests

(10 minutes)

Share your prayer requests with other family members. Volunteer to pray specifically for one other person during the coming week.

My prayer request is _____

_____

and _____ is praying for me.

I am praying for _____ and his/her prayer request is _____

_____

_____.

LARGE GROUP

A Word of Hope

(10 minutes)

When we come face to face with the stark rebellion in our souls, we are ready to enter the process of deep healing, because we recognize our ongoing need for repentance and grace. When we are prepared to confess our antidependence, the words of the Apostle Paul come with sweetness to our souls:

> **For he [God] has rescued us from the dominion of darkness and brought us into the kingdom of the Son he loves, in whom we have redemption, the forgiveness of sins. (Colossians 1:13-14)**

Rejoice in your forgiveness!

Prayer

All who wish may join in repeating the Serenity Prayer.

During the Week

Make a list in your journal of your complaints against God—what you wish He would do or would have done on your behalf. (This exercise may trigger memories of how you felt when past events turned anticipation into disappointment.) Write whether and how your anger became a determination to enthrone yourself in God's place.

For more information on this week's topic, see *From Bondage to Bonding*, chapter 10. For more information regarding next week's topic, read chapter 12.

Benediction

Hear the words of the Apostle Paul:

> **May the grace of the Lord Jesus Christ, and the love of God, and the fellowship of the Holy Spirit be with you all. (2 Corinthians 13:14)**

Thinking God's Thoughts

Theme for meditation: GOD REIGNS.

Reading: Exodus 15:11-18
Isaiah 6:1-7
Psalm 146:1-10
Proverbs 14:12
Matthew 20:20-28
Revelation 19:4-10

Prayer:
Lord, thank You for this evidence in Your Word of Your holiness and majesty:
Lord, I confess these areas in my life where I have tried to rule in Your place:
Lord, this is what I will do (or stop doing) to allow You to be God over my life:

NOTE

1. C. S. Lewis, *The Lion, the Witch and the Wardrobe* (New York: Collier Books, 1950), pages 75-76.

RECEIVING, NOT ACHIEVING

Welcome. As you proceed into a deeper understanding of what it means to drop your codependent strategies and live by grace, may the Father be close to comfort you and to assure you of His unfailing love.

Warm-up
(5 minutes)
1. Turn to someone near you and describe a gift you were able to receive during the past two weeks. (It may have been the gift of a hug, a favor, forgiveness, or an unexpected kindness.)

> Read this section to yourself, and write answers to the questions that follow.
> (20 minutes)

Loving Our Autonomy

As we move into grief for our love losses and into repentance for our love failures, it becomes increasingly evident that we cannot manage our lives according to our old codependent strategies. We must turn to God for the help we need that can come only from beyond our own limited resources.

But even as we admit our need for help from God, we must also struggle with the reality that in our deepest hearts we hate to give up our autonomy. We go back and forth between longing for intimacy with God while at the same time despising the horror of depending utterly on Him alone. We know we should love Him and sometimes we do. But we're also enraged because He has disappointed us, and we don't want to trust Him again. We even (probably unconsciously) hate Him for demanding that we love others in spite of our having been wounded so badly ourselves.

Even for codependents committed to recovery it's not easy to recognize or acknowledge the entrenched outrage in our souls. Ultimately, however, only a heart deeply gripped by the reality of its rebellion against a good and loving God can be open to the miracle of grace. Until we face how wicked that rebellion is in God's eyes, we will continue to live life on our terms, not God's, and our raised fists will keep out the gift of grace God says is our only way to renewed fellowship with Him.

We have tried to find life without Him and have failed. Our codependent strategies haven't ushered us into anything but emptiness and frustration. We've pursued self-protection long enough to know there is no real life there. As frightening and painful as it is to repent of and turn from our autonomy, we know we can't experience the grace and sufficiency of God any other way. And unless we repent of our anger against Him and our sinful attempts to make life work without Him, we will not taste the grace we so desperately need.

2. What did you discover when you wrote in your journal your complaints against God this week? How did you feel? Was it hard to do or easy?

3. If you can, describe an event or situation in your life that "forced" you to turn to God for help.

4. What did you do to try to "fix" that disaster? How did that work?

5. What might be (or might have been) God's deeper purpose in allowing that disaster to happen?

6. What were your dominant feelings toward God and others during that time?

FAMILY GROUP

Needing and Receiving God's Forgiveness

Briefly talk about how you are feeling right now. Then read and discuss the next section together.
(15 minutes)

Ever since the first rebellion of Adam and Eve, mankind's greatest relational need has been for forgiveness. We have spurned God-dependence and violated mutual inter-dependence, we have shaken our demanding fists in God's face, and without forgiveness we are doomed to perish in our loneliness and rage.

When we consider that codependency is basically self-focused, it's clear that developing a "false self" has kept us from genuinely loving God and others. Our layers of self-protection and our antidependence toward God make all of us legitimately and truly guilty—for our failure to love God and others, and for our angry demands that everyone, including God, do what we want. Our greatest grace imperative is for forgiveness in the face of our refusal to trust God (self-sufficiency) and our failure to love others (self-preoccupation). We think those who have harmed us need forgiveness more than we do, but the irrefutable fact is that we, too, have sinned miserably and stand in desperate need of grace.

God's "solution" for our sin problem is not somehow to get us to work harder to obey His command to love Him and others. Rather, He calls us to admit we have not done and cannot do what He commands—our fallen nature makes it impossible. In the face of that impossibility to be perfect, we are left with the ultimate choice: despair or grace.

It is precisely in the darkness of our utter helplessness that the wonder of God's grace dawns on our souls with its greatest beauty. What we cannot do for ourselves (earn God's favor by striving to be good), Jesus Christ accomplished for us by paying the penalty of our sin on the Cross and offering us His righteousness in exchange. God's forgiveness of those who put their faith in the substitutionary death of His Son, Jesus, is the essence of the gospel of grace. Grace refers to God's kindness directed toward those who believe in Jesus. That forgiving grace is undeserved, unearned, and unrepayable. The "Power greater than ourselves"—the God of the Bible—has restored us to more than sanity; He has restored us to the fellowship with Himself for which we were created, returning us to our full humanness once again. Those who refuse His forgiving grace miss life.

7. Most of us find it tough to receive grace consistently. What makes it tough for you to receive grace instead of working harder to love right?

FAMILY GROUP

> Remain together to read this section and work through the study of Jesus' story of the prodigal son.
> (30 minutes)

Embracing Grace

A third and crucial kind of grace necessary and available to us as recovering codependents is God's *embracing grace* for dealing with our spirit of antidependence. This is perhaps the most unexpected grace of all, because our fist in God's face leaves us altogether deserving of His righteous judgment. This grace is best illustrated in Jesus' parable of the prodigal son, found in Luke 15:11-32.

> **"There was a man who had two sons. The younger one said to his father, 'Father, give me my share of the estate.' So he divided his property between them." (Luke 15:11-12)**

Kenneth E. Bailey, who lived in the Middle East and researched peasant life there, illuminates the cultural setting of this parable in his book *Poet and Peasant*. According to Mr. Bailey, the prodigal's request for his share of his father's inheritance, coming when his father was still in good health, shows that the prodigal wished for his father's death—a profound break of relationship between father and son. Moreover, the older son's silent agreement to share the inheritance implies that he agreed with his brother.

8. What might the father have felt in this situation?

> **"Not long after that, the younger son got together all he had, set off for a distant country and there squandered his wealth in wild living. After he had spent everything, there was a severe famine in that whole country, and he began to be in need. So he went and hired himself out to a citizen of that country, who sent him to his fields to feed pigs. He longed to fill his stomach with the pods that the pigs were eating, but no one gave him anything.**
>
> **"When he came to his senses, he said, 'How many of my father's hired men have food to spare, and here I am starving to death! I will set out and go back to my father and say to him: Father, I have sinned against heaven and against you. I am no longer worthy to be called your son; make me like one of your hired men.'" (Luke 15:13-19)**

After the prodigal descended from prosperity into poverty, he "came to his senses" (verse 17) and decided to return home. However, he "repented" only of squandering his father's money, not of breaking his father's heart. He intended to earn money by becoming a hired servant, saving enough to pay his father back so his father would not disown him. Also, a hired servant was a free man with his own income living independently in the local village, so the prodigal could maintain his pride and his independence.

9. Why would the father be pleased or displeased with his son's plan to become a hired servant and pay him back?

10. Do you have anything in common with this son's view of his father and his own solution for his predicament? If so, what?

> **"So he got up and went to his father.**
>
> **"But while he was still a long way off, his father saw him and was filled with compassion for him; he ran to his son, threw his arms around him and kissed him.**
>
> **"The son said to him, 'Father, I have sinned against heaven and**

against you. I am no longer worthy to be called your son.'

"But the father said to his servants, 'Quick! Bring the best robe and put it on him. Put a ring on his finger and sandals on his feet. Bring the fattened calf and kill it. Let's have a feast and celebrate. For this son of mine was dead and is alive again; he was lost and is found.' So they began to celebrate." (Luke 15:20-24)

When the prodigal's father humiliated himself by running to meet his son (Oriental noblemen *never* run), embracing him instead of disowning him, he revealed a grace that longs more for relationship than restitution. The prodigal was drawn to genuine repentance and grace—not when he recognized his foolishness, but when he received his father's welcoming grace—and abandoned his self-sufficient offer to become a hired servant.

11. How does it affect you to know that God longs for a restored relationship with you, not repayment?

"Meanwhile, the older son was in the field. When he came near the house, he heard music and dancing. So he called one of the servants and asked him what was going on. 'Your brother has come,' he replied, 'and your father has killed the fattened calf because he has him back safe and sound.'

"The older brother became angry and refused to go in. So his father went out and pleaded with him. But he answered his father, 'Look! All these years I've been slaving for you and never disobeyed your orders. Yet you never gave me even a young goat so I could celebrate with my friends. But when this son of yours who has squandered your property with prostitutes comes home, you kill the fattened calf for him!'

"'My son,' the father said, 'you are always with me, and everything I have is yours. But we had to celebrate and be glad, because this brother of yours was dead and is alive again; he was lost and is found.'" (Luke 15:25-32)

Unfortunately, the older brother was more resistant to grace. His public insult of his father (by refusing to join the party) put him as much in need of repentance and grace as the prodigal had been. When the father humiliated himself a second time by coming out to plead for his older son to be reconciled with both his brother and his father, the older son angrily complained that his "servanthood" over the years had gained him nothing of what he really wanted—which was not relationship with his father but the opportunity to party with his friends.

12. How did this son misread his father's heart toward both him and his brother?

13. a. With which character in this story do you most identify? Why?

b. What does this tell you about your own understanding of the heart of God?

14. Why is God's embracing grace so crucial for you?

Prayer Requests

(10 minutes)

Share your prayer requests with other family members. Volunteer to pray specifically for one other person during the coming week.

My prayer request is _____

_____

and _____ is praying for me.

I am praying for _____ and his/her prayer request is _____

_____

_____.

![LARGE GROUP]

A Word of Hope

(10 minutes)

Perhaps the most wonderful and yet most difficult-to-accept aspect of grace is that it cannot be achieved. It is both comforting and humiliating to realize that nothing in us can merit God's blessings.

If we will receive instead of try to achieve, we will find God's embracing grace utterly dependable.

The Apostle John reassures us,

> **Yet to all who *received* him [Jesus], to those who believed in his name, he gave the right to become children of God. (John 1:12, emphasis added)**

Prayer

Those who wish may repeat the Lord's Prayer, focusing on God as our perfect heavenly Father.

During the Week

Write in your journal answers to these questions:

- How have you wounded the heart of God by your attitude toward Him?

- Considering the gifts the father in Jesus' parable offered the repentant prodigal and the older son, how would you feel and behave differently if you believed God longs to treat you like the father treated his two sons?

If you're not sure you've ever actually confessed your sin to God and asked Jesus to be your Savior, consider doing that this week. Tell a friend about it.

For more information on this week's topic, see *From Bondage to Bonding,* chapter 12. For more information regarding next week's topic, read chapter 13.

Benediction

Listen to the words of the Apostle Jude:

> **To him who is able to keep you from falling and to present you before his glorious presence without fault and with great joy—to the only God our Savior be glory, majesty, power and authority, through Jesus Christ our Lord, before all ages, now and forevermore! Amen. (Jude 24-25)**

Thinking God's Thoughts

Theme for meditation: GOD EMBRACES THE UNDESERVING.

Reading: Deuteronomy 7:7-11, 9:5
    Jeremiah 31:31-34
    Psalm 103:6-12
    Job 42:1-6,10-12
    Matthew 20:1-16
    Romans 5:1-8

Prayer:
 Father, thank You for this evidence in Your Word that You love the undeserving:
 Father, thank You for this evidence in my life that You love me though I'm
  undeserving:
 Father, this is what I will do (or stop doing) to repent of my demandingness
  toward You:

GOD AS FATHER

LARGE GROUP

We've been dealing with the topic of grace, an essential landmark in our recovery process. Grace demands nothing of us in payment, but everything of us in trust. Our entire way of life is threatened when we depend on God's grace alone. This session will examine the benefits and responsibilities of radical God-dependence.

Warm-up
(5 minutes)

1. Tell someone from your family group something your mother or father did *right* as parents.

FAMILY GROUP

> Read aloud this section and discuss the questions.
> (15 minutes)

Turning to God

When we consider our desperate need for grace throughout our recovery process and beyond—especially forgiving grace for our failure to love God and others—we begin to recognize that without God our lives are hopeless. Often we're appalled by that recognition, ashamed that we've not been able to maintain our self-sufficiency. We're drowning and need a savior, but we're embarrassed at our inability to save ourselves. Of course our embarrassment is irrelevant—we need help, like it or not. But our shame can keep us from asking for and receiving that help—or being grateful for it.

Genuine recovery from codependency is found not in freeing ourselves from needing, but in receiving grace. The cost of our freedom is radical dependence on God, which flies in the face of our self-reliance and autonomy. In fact, God at times allows us to get in over our heads just to show us our need for Him. Unless we're driven to dependence, we will not experience grace.

The first two steps in the AA recovery program express our willingness to renounce our recurring self-reliance. The third step speaks of surrender to and dependence on God, affirming that *we made a decision to turn our will and our lives over to the care of God as we understood him.* We codependents typically insist that we remain strictly in control of our lives, and it requires a major shift in life strategy for us to relinquish that control to the care of God.

However, if we're to put God in charge of our will and life, we ought to be asking what kind of God He is. Can He be trusted to really *care* for us, as this step suggests?

2. What part of AA's Step Three can you affirm?

3. What experience, if any, have you had with God that would make you hesitate to take Step Three wholeheartedly?

ON YOUR OWN

Read this section individually, and write answers to the questions in the space provided. (20 minutes)

What Is God Like?

Ever since the Garden of Eden Satan has tried to slander God's character, and he often succeeds because of our parents' failures. We receive our earliest and most profoundly believed ideas about God through watching our parents, particularly our fathers. A child who grows up with a distant, unresponsive, or unpleasable father believes God is like that, too. Worse than that, parents who abuse or neglect their children cause those children to view God as harsh and vindictive (perhaps even evil). This may keep them from even wanting a relationship with God as adults. If we are to take Step Three and turn our will and lives over to God's care, we must discover what God is really like.

We can't fashion God into whatever shape suits our fancy. He is who He is, and He reveals who He is and what He's like in the Bible. Reading about God may not change our emotions toward Him, but the Bible can show us where the truth about God (what Scripture says about Him) contradicts what we feel about God (based on our childhood misconceptions) so we can make responsible choices about what to believe and how to act in relationship to Him.

Nowhere is God's nature seen more clearly than in the life of Jesus, God's Son made flesh to dwell among us. By observing Jesus' words and actions in the gospels we glimpse the wonderful goodness, justice, and grace of our Father God. Jesus Himself declared, "Anyone who has seen me has seen the Father" (John 14:9). If we want our misconceptions about God cleared up, we would do well to look at Jesus.

Moreover, because of Jesus' sacrificial death to pay for our sins, we can now enter a redeemed Parent-child relationship with God, seeing ourselves as His beloved children and practicing a childlike relationship with Him. Good fathers interact with their children in ways that affirm their children's value as human beings, just as God in Scripture interacted with His children and continues to interact with us even today. Young children have nothing to offer but themselves—their need, their trust, and their love—and God meets our need, deserves our trust, and enjoys our love like the good Father He is.

4. In what ways do you wish your father had been different toward you?

5. What false ideas of God do you think you got from observing your parents?

6. In what ways, if any, did your father reflect what God is really like?

7. In what ways do you relate to God as you relate to your earthly father?

8. How do these Scripture passages reveal God to be similar to or different from your father?

> **You saw how the LORD your God carried you, as a father carries his son, all the way you went until you reached this place. (Deuteronomy 1:31)**

> **As a father has compassion on his children,**
>   **so the LORD has compassion on those who fear him;**
> **for he knows how we are formed,**
>   **he remembers that we are dust. (Psalm 103:13-14)**

FAMILY GROUP

Join your family group to read the next section and discuss the questions that follow.
(30 minutes)

The Perfect Father

What is God like as our good Father? First, He is *just*. Parents who fail to set or enforce high standards do their children great damage. Children want their parents to do right, and they're disappointed and embarrassed when their parents are morally lax—

toward themselves or toward their children. Kids thrive on discipline, not permissiveness. When God stands in the way of our foolishness, we should feel loved, sensing from Him not hatred but concern, not vengeance but compassion. He loves us too much to let our continued rebellion (which would ultimately destroy us) go unchallenged.

God is also *loving,* like a good father who accepts and delights in his child. One of the most profound effects of being deeply connected to God is a renewed sense of our own preciousness. Children place value on whatever their parents value; that is why parental neglect or abuse is so devastating to a child's self-esteem. Self-worth is a byproduct that flows from being loved; children can't generate it themselves. But when we believe God cherishes us as beloved children, we can believe in our worth as persons. As we experience God's steady love and delight in us as His precious children, we begin to place that same value on ourselves. We are children of the Great King and special to our Father. Princes and princesses don't let themselves be abused; they like themselves and expect to be respected.

Loved children also know they'll be received and forgiven when they repent of any wrongdoing. As the prodigal son in Jesus' parable was embraced by his father, so our heavenly Father longs to embrace us every time we return to Him.

Those codependents whose fathers disappointed them may find it difficult to turn their will and lives over to God's care. But as we correct our misconceptions about Him through a study of Scripture and time spent quietly in His presence, we'll grow to trust Him more and to find an increasing freedom to be authentic—to experience, perhaps for the first time, what it's like to rest in the arms of a good Father who cares deeply for us and is committed to our good.

9. Does the thought of God's justice frighten or encourage you? Why?

10. How does your experience of parental discipline make you feel when you read that "the LORD disciplines those he loves, as a father the son he delights in" (Proverbs 3:12)? Why?

11. If you can, tell about a time you experienced God *delighting* in you as His loved child.

12. What would be different in your life if you deeply believed God was delighted with you just because you are His son or daughter?

13. Tell why it is difficult or easy for you to just spend time alone in God's presence.

14.   a. What does a child offer his or her parent?

      b. What does this teach us about our relationship to God as our Father?

FAMILY GROUP

Prayer Requests
(10 minutes)
Share your prayer requests with other family members. Volunteer to pray specifically for one other person during the coming week.

My prayer request is _____

_____

and _____ is praying for me.

I am praying for _____ and his/her prayer request is _____

_____

_____.

LARGE GROUP

A Word of Hope
(10 minutes)
The prophet Zephaniah offers this promise concerning our Father God:

155

The LORD your God is with you,
 he is mighty to save.
He will take great delight in you,
 he will quiet you with his love,
 he will rejoice over you with singing. (Zephaniah 3:17)

Take comfort in those words this week.

Prayer

Those who wish may repeat the Lord's Prayer, concentrating on the blessings that are ours because God is our heavenly Father.

During the Week

In session 4 you started thinking about what you longed for from your parents. Weeks later, you may be much more aware of the losses you've suffered. Take about thirty minutes of uninterrupted time to make a further list of what you longed for from your parents—first your father, then your mother—remaining as open as possible to the grief you might feel. Share this list and your reaction with someone you trust.

For more information on this week's and next week's topic, see *From Bondage to Bonding,* chapter 13.

Benediction

Hear the ancient priestly blessing:

The LORD bless you
 and keep you;
the LORD make his face shine upon you
 and be gracious to you;
the LORD turn his face toward you
 and give you peace. (Numbers 6:24-26)

Thinking God's Thoughts

Theme for meditation: GOD IS OUR HEAVENLY FATHER.

Reading: Deuteronomy 1:19-31
                 Zephaniah 3:14-17
                 Psalm 103:13-22
                 Proverbs 3:11-12
                 Luke 11:9-13
                 Romans 8:12-17

Prayer:
      Father, thank You for this evidence in Your Word that You are a good Father:
      Father, thank You for this evidence in my life that You've adopted me into
         Your family:
      Father, this is what I will do (or stop doing) to act like Your child, not Your
         slave or employee:

GOD-DEPENDENCE

This is the final session dealing with the process of recovery from our codependent bondage. Next week will begin the final six-week section dealing with what biblical bonding looks like.

Warm-up
(5 minutes)

1. Tell another person one obstacle you have had to overcome in making it to these meetings each week. Congratulate each other on the accomplishment.

> Read this section to yourself and complete the exercises.
> (20 minutes)

Declaration of Dependence

Because we were made for relationship with God, we as recovering codependents "come home" to our true selves when we turn our lives over to the care of our heavenly Father. Just as children in healthy homes lean wholeheartedly and unself-consciously on their parents, so we, too, must increasingly surrender ourselves to God and depend on Him for all that we need.

God-dependence may mean different things to different people. Consider this definition:

> God-dependence means that a person enters life through faith in Christ's substitute death for him or her. It also means that a person sustains life by daily living in repentance and grace (God's acceptance, forgiveness, and empowerment). This results in spiritual vitality, a sense of place and worth, and the potential for intimacy.

What does it mean to enter life through surrender to God? When a person receives God's gift of forgiveness through faith in Christ's death on his behalf, that person moves from Death into Life. Connectedness with God always means life, and separation from Him always means death. When we enter renewed fellowship with God through faith in Christ, we have within us the Life Jesus had in Him, the Life of God. Codependency is a way of life, but confessing our sin and accepting God's gift of salvation offers us Life itself, allowing us to reclaim our true humanity.

It's easy to say that real life comes only from God, but it's not always easy to believe it. If we've never tasted that kind of life, we have every reason to doubt that it could be as terrific as the Bible claims. And since God never promises that real life will feel good in the short run, we're taking a big risk putting all of our eggs in God's basket. Often the only reason we give up and give God a chance is that we're desperate and out of other options.

2. Choose one of your typical codependent strategies for depending on yourself instead of on God, and tell how that strategy has kept you from being alive in your relationships.

3. Life must have nourishment in order to thrive (or even survive). What have you done in the past week to nourish your life in Christ?

4. If you have trouble investing time in your friendship with Christ, what do you suppose blocks you from making that a priority?

Meet together to read and discuss this section.
(20 minutes)

FAMILY GROUP

Surrender to His Life

We sustain our spiritual life by abiding daily in grace (God's acceptance, forgiveness, and empowerment through the Holy Spirit). When we confess our sin and believe Jesus' death paid for those sins, we receive not just God's help but God's very Life. That Life in turn will be expressed through our individual, unique, redeemed personalities and gifts as we spend time with God and live in obedience to His will. Bible reading, prayer, worship, time with other believers, and the sacraments all convey grace to us, but it is God's Holy Spirit operating in our spirit through those things that makes us truly alive.

Jesus is our model for God-dependent living. His every word and action had its foundation in reliance on His Father. The intimate fellowship He enjoyed with God was the wellspring out of which flowed the grace He offered to those He encountered. The Son of God, who had Life in Himself (John 1:4), was nevertheless utterly dependent on the Father's Life in Him to know what to say and how to act. We're called to depend on God in the same way.

5. Someone has said God doesn't want to be our spare tire but our engine and steering wheel. Can you think of any times during the past week when you experienced God as your engine, having Him *live through* you, not just *help* you in a crisis? Describe the situation.

159

6. How, if at all, has God been your steering wheel recently? (In other words, in what way did He reveal His will to you and/or enable you to carry out His will?)

7. What do you find hard about making God your engine and steering wheel?

8. Think of the most unsettling decision regarding relationships you might have to make during the next few weeks—perhaps a confrontation or an acknowledgment of sin or a change in what you will allow to happen in a relationship. How would your dependence on God enable you to make and carry out that decision with greater courage?

FAMILY GROUP

<table>
<tr><td>Remain together for this section.
(25 minutes)</td></tr>
</table>

Belonging and Loving

Surrendering our will and life to God—though He is utterly reliable because of His unchanging character—is a dangerous way to live. If we depend on God and Him alone, we must turn and face everything we've run from as codependents all our lives. We must ask for what our souls long for instead of protecting ourselves from the pain of its loss. We must embrace the terror of aloneness, the possibility that no one will understand or approve of us except God. We must release our attempts to control the people and circumstances of our lives, freeing others to respond positively or negatively—or not at all—without medicating our pain. It will demand of us a trust that must itself come from God.

However, the more we depend on God to sustain our inner lives, the more secure we'll feel and the more we'll have to offer to others. Becoming precious children of God through our faith in Christ gives us a sense of belonging and worth (John 1:12). We don't have to "earn our keep"; we have an uncontested place in Christ's family because we've been bought with His blood. Instead of trying desperately to manage the people and circumstances in our world, we can accept Jesus' gracious invitation: "Come to me, all you who are weary and burdened, and I will give you rest" (Matthew 11:28). How wonderful to rest in Jesus' care and turn our frantic busyness over to Him, knowing He will work all things for our ultimate good as we become more like Him (Romans 8:28-29).

Our relationships with others can also change when God's Life dwells in us, freeing us to embrace genuine intimacy. Our deepest fear of abandonment—that God might disown us—will, because of Calvary, never happen. So we can risk being who we really are with other people. Even if we're rejected by others, we can rest in knowing we're accepted by the Father. Rejection will hurt, but we really will survive if we lean on Him. Depending utterly on God for our ultimate well-being is the doorway to intimacy—to a renewed freedom to love, to hurt, to laugh, to make mistakes, to ask forgiveness, to feel our feelings, to start each day new. We're free in Him to finally be alive.

But with freedom comes responsibility. God hasn't freed us to become self-centered. He calls us out of codependent bondage so we can bond with others in mutual interdependence. Surrendering to God requires that we own our responsibility to love others well. He offers us grace so we can risk offering that same grace to others.

9. Consider this partial list of choices God might ask you to make in His strength during the coming month. Have each group member tell which are the most terrifying for him or her and why.

- To turn and face your pain
- To live without medicating your pain
- To ask for what your soul longs for
- To become willing to be alone with God
- To become willing to be misunderstood
- To become willing to be disapproved
- To become willing to be rejected
- To give up control over someone you love

10. Imagine being asked to walk the length of a sturdy plank ten inches wide and twelve feet long.

- If it were placed on the floor in the center of your group, would you be willing to walk the plank?

- If it were raised to a height of five feet off the ground, would you be willing to walk the plank?

- If it were suspended 1000 feet off the ground, would you be willing to walk the plank?

11. The difference between these exercises is the degree of danger involved: Few would be injured walking along the floor; more serious damage could occur in a five-foot fall; death would probably result from a thousand-foot fall. The greater your fear of negative consequences, the less willing you would be to take the risk.

Apply this principle to the answer you gave in question 9. If you fear that making one of those choices would result in your emotional or relational death, you probably won't take the risk. Discuss with your family group whether the following statement is true for you, and why:

Because God's love and acceptance of me is utterly reliable, other people's rejection or disapproval has power to hurt me (a five-foot drop), but it won't destroy me (a thousand-foot drop); therefore, I can risk moving toward them without demanding that they not let me down.

Prayer Requests

(10 minutes)
Share your prayer requests with other family members. Volunteer to pray specifically for one other person during the coming week.

My prayer request is _____

_____

and _____ is praying for me.

I am praying for _____ and his/her prayer request is _____

_____

_____.

A Word of Hope

(10 minutes)
Depending on God offers us *Life* in the deepest sense of the word. Moses urged the Israelites:

> **Now choose life, so that you and your children may live and that you may love the LORD your God, listen to his voice, and hold fast to him. For the LORD is your life. (Deuteronomy 30:19-20)**

Prayer

All who wish may join in repeating the Serenity Prayer.

During the Week

In your journal, write a letter to God telling Him about a risk you need to take, how you feel about it, and what you'd like Him to do.

For more information on this week's topic, see *From Bondage to Bonding,* chapter 13. For more information regarding next week's topic, read chapter 14.

Benediction

Receive these words of comfort from the Apostle Peter:

The God of all grace, who called you to his eternal glory in Christ, after you have suffered a little while, will himself restore you and make you strong, firm and steadfast. To him be the power for ever and ever. Amen. (1 Peter 5:10-11)

Thinking God's Thoughts

Theme for meditation: GOD IS OUR LIFE.

Reading: Deuteronomy 30:11-20
Ezekiel 37:1-14
Psalm 16:1-11
Proverbs 8:1-4,32-36
John 5:16-30,39-40
Colossians 3:1-4

Prayer:
Father, thank You for this evidence in Your Word that Life is found in You:
Father, thank You for these areas in my life where You have made me come alive:
Father, this is what I will do (or stop doing) to live out Your life in me:

PART FOUR

MUTUAL INTERDEPENDENCE

MUTUAL LOVE

When God brings us out of the bondage of our codependency through the process of grief and grace into God-dependence, He also calls us to the bonding of mutual interdependence. This session begins our consideration of what interdependence is.

Warm-up

(5 minutes)

1. Tell one other person about a risk you took this past week, including what the outcome was and how you felt.

> Read this section aloud and discuss the questions that follow.
> (20 minutes)

Detachment

Interdependence is what we long for in our relationships, and we want it to be mutual—both partners moving toward each other with love, respect, and freedom. Mutual interdependence, however, is based on this crucial assumption: *Each partner in the relationship is a separate person taking full responsibility for personal choices.* Sometimes that establishment of self-hood develops through a process called *detachment.*

Detachment refers to a codependent's temporary emotional distancing from an enmeshed relationship in order to examine what is making the relationship unhealthy. Detachment may look like, and may in fact become, antidependence unless its goal is ultimately to reattach in an appropriate way and to learn to love correctly. To detach, codependents must invite others (in a support group, for example) to help them gain perspective on and grieve over how they have failed to genuinely love.

Love can't flourish in the presence of unchallenged abuse or addiction. Parents, spouses, and friends who by their action or inaction enable their loved ones to remain in their addictions are not operating out of love, but out of bondage to their own codependent behavior. Their enabling flows from their fear of confrontation and loss, not from their commitment to the other's ultimate good.

Detachment involves a codependent's decision to confront the addict's behavior and to refuse the abuse that has accompanied it. In some cases it may include physically leaving a relationship for a season to break the abusive cycle. However, abandoning the relationship, although relief from the pain in the relationship may be tempting, might not be the right (loving) thing to do. Many enablers run from their enmeshed relationships to free themselves from dysfunction, refusing to face their own love failures and ignoring the deeper issues of their autonomy and God's claim on their loving obedience. Moreover, they often discover later that the problem wasn't the addict, but their own wrong way of relating to the addict. The codependent's relational pattern won't be changed by leaving; it will simply reappear in future relationships if it isn't dealt with.

2. Think of how you have experienced being enmeshed in a relationship (enabling others in their addiction, feeling others' pain more than your own, minimizing others' wrongs, etc.). In what ways have you practiced (or could you practice) detaching emotionally from those enmeshed relationships? In other words, how can you stop enabling, learn to feel your own pain, confront others in love, stop letting yourself be abused, etc.?

3. How has meeting with this group helped you detach appropriately?

4. Tell how you are or are not growing in being a separate person taking responsibility for your own choices.

5. How have you practiced reattaching appropriately with others, especially in your committed relationships? If you haven't done that yet, how does it feel to think about doing that?

ON YOUR OWN

Individually, read this section and answer the questions in the space provided.
(20 minutes)

Reciprocal Grace

Our redeemed nature as children of God draws us to love others as we love ourselves, and we reach toward that new nature when we move through detachment into mutual interdependence. The grace offered us through our dependence on God bonds us to Him and becomes ours to offer others; if they choose, they can bond with us, too. But we cannot force our way. As we move from bondage to bonding, we must realize that bonding is a mysterious union requiring (in adults) two consenting partners. Consider this definition of mutual interdependence:

> Mutual interdependence occurs when two persons, secure in God's acceptance, mutually give and receive love and forgiveness, without demanding approval or conformity to expectations in return. This results in spiritual vitality, a balanced view of self, and genuine intimacy.

Mutual interdependence happens best in the context of two persons who are secure in their status before God and no longer need to demand that the other change or approve of them. They love not from deficit but from an abundance of grace.

It won't be easy, of course. In the vacuum left by our abandoned strategies of self-protection and control, we must risk believing God's acceptance is enough for us in the absence of approval from people. Our aloneness with God will both exhilarate and terrify. Our neediness will feel like death, and the challenge will be to act on the reality that it is, in fact, Life.

6. List ways you expect/demand of the most important person(s) in your life either approval and/or conformity to your expectations. Try to be specific.

I want _____ to approve of this in me:

I want _____ to do this:

7. How do you *feel* when the approval or conformity does not happen?

8. What do you generally *do* when the approval or conformity does not happen?

9. What would be different in your behavior if you *desired* but did not *demand* the other person's approval or conformity?

FAMILY GROUP

Rejoin your family group to
read the next section.
(5 minutes)

Mutual Love

Crucial to a balanced view of mutual interdependence is our ability to determine our
own legitimate responsibility—neither giving too much nor too little in any

relationship. Feedback from a support group helps us learn give-and-take in our relationships, based on what is good for both ourselves and the people we are learning to love in a more biblical way.

Love is the first mutually enjoyed gift of interdependence. Some think love refers to romantic feelings, but if limited to that, many of us would conclude that our relationships are doomed because none of those feelings are left after years of abuse and disappointment. Love, however, is not ultimately an emotion but a commitment to pursue aggressively what is for the other person's good, a choice we make to act in someone else's best interest. God requires us to love our neighbors as ourselves—not to create in ourselves more loving feelings toward them, but to determine what is in their best interest and then do it.

As recovering codependents we express our love in two ways. First, we discontinue the codependent behaviors on which we've built our lives. We can stop our *denial* by facing what is in our souls and being who we really are without pretense about our pain or our sin. We can abandon our *self-sufficiency* and admit we need God and others in order to live fully. Our *control strategies* can give way to letting others make their own choices and live with the consequences of those choices. We can renounce our *self-contempt* and our willingness to be *helpless, opinionless, and choiceless*, offering the substance of our souls to bless the ones we're committed to loving. If we're connected to God and leaning desperately on Him, we can stop doing codependent things.

Second, we can practice Christlike behaviors even when we don't particularly feel like it. This doesn't mean we ignore our negative feelings, but that we acknowledge them with integrity and intensity, and then choose to behave as God directs us through His Word and Spirit. That's what Jesus did in the Garden of Gethsemane when He told His disciples, "My soul is overwhelmed with sorrow to the point of death," then cried out to God, "Take this cup from me. Yet not what I will, but what you will" (Mark 14:34,36).

The Apostle Paul told the believers in Colosse:

As God's chosen people, holy and dearly loved, clothe yourselves with compassion, kindness, humility, gentleness and patience. (Colossians 3:12)

As redeemed codependents we can put on *compassion* toward other people's pain because we've learned to linger in our own. We can practice *kindness* because we no longer have to punish or control those who have disappointed us. We recognize that *humility* consists not in denying our power but in acknowledging that it comes from God. *Gentleness* is possible even when rebuking those who harm us, because we know our purpose is not to destroy but to redeem. And *patience* becomes our habit because we know God isn't finished with us yet, and because His presence enables us to endure our fiery trials with perseverance, if not always tranquility. Because Christ dwells within us, we can choose to act like Him.

ON YOUR OWN

> Work individually on this exercise.
> (15 minutes)

10. Write a specific example of how you could do each "putting off" and each "putting on" behavior listed here. (For example, we put off lying to ourselves by no longer pretending that unkind words don't hurt, or we put on compassion by listening to someone's sorrow without trying to fix it or give advice.)

PUT OFF
Lying to ourselves

Relying only on ourselves

Believing we have more power than we have

Holding ourselves in contempt

Giving all control and decisions to others

PUT ON
Compassion

Kindness

Humility

Gentleness

Patience

FAMILY GROUP

Discuss your answers to question 10.
(5 minutes)

11. Do you feel able to do the things you listed, or will you need to seek grace?

Prayer Requests

(10 minutes)

Share your prayer requests with other family members. Volunteer to pray specifically for one other person during the coming week.

My prayer request is _____

_____

and _____ is praying for me.

I am praying for _____ and his/her prayer request is _____

_____

_____.

LARGE GROUP

A Word of Hope
(10 minutes)

Our recovery journey out of the bondage of codependency and into the bonding of mutual interdependence is a life-long process. Listen to these encouraging words of the Apostle Paul:

> **He who began a good work in you will carry it on to completion until the day of Christ Jesus. (Philippians 1:6)**

Prayer
All who wish may join in repeating the Serenity Prayer.

During the Week
Ask God to enable you to do one of the things you listed in question 10. Record in your journal what happens then, and how you feel about it. Do you feel more self-contempt when you fail at compassion or patience? Do you feel more proud of your control over yourself when you succeed?

For more information on this week's and next week's topic, see *From Bondage to Bonding,* chapter 14.

Benediction
Hear the words of the Apostle Paul:

> **May the grace of the Lord Jesus Christ, and the love of God, and the fellowship of the Holy Spirit be with you all. (2 Corinthians 13:14)**

Thinking God's Thoughts
Theme for meditation: GOD IS COMMITTED TO OUR GOOD.

Reading: Genesis 50:15-21
             Jeremiah 29:4-14
             Psalm 119:65-72
             Proverbs 2:1-11
             John 3:1-21
             Hebrews 11:8-16

Prayer:
    Father, thank You for this evidence in Your Word that Your love is directed
        toward my good:
    Father, thank You for these areas in my life where I've seen Your good intentions:
    Father, this is what I will do (or stop doing) to love (do good to) those
        around me:

MUTUAL FORGIVENESS

Escaping codependency and embracing biblical love means that from a position of inner connectedness with God we offer one another the gift of love without demanding in return approval or conformity to our expectations. That was the topic of our last session. A second precious gift we offer each other when we become mutually interdependent is forgiveness—the heartbeat of any love relationship. Forgiveness has three essential ingredients, which are the topic of this week's meeting.

Warm-up
(5 minutes)
1. Turn to someone near you and share one "putting on" or "putting off" exercise you did since your last session. How did it go? How do you feel about that?

> Individually, read this section and answer the questions.
> (20 minutes)

Loving Confrontation
The first ingredient of forgiveness in a mutually interdependent relationship is loving confrontation—communicating to others the impact of their sin on us. We've always considered it unloving (and certainly dangerous) to risk genuine honesty about how others have damaged or abused us. It's safer to take the blame, swallow the hurt, and just "forgive and forget." But it's more loving—and more respectful—to set appropriate boundaries by refusing to accept mistreatment; it's good not just for ourselves but for our abusers as well. A recovering codependent who says without apology, "You may not mistreat me anymore!" is loving well because abuse damages both victim and agent. However, setting boundaries is consistent with biblical love only if the focus is

175

on mutual welfare, not revenge or personal safety.

Forgiveness and restoration are impossible if sin is not addressed. Jesus didn't forgive without confrontation and a call to repentance. "Repent, for the kingdom of heaven is near," Jesus preached (Matthew 4:17). He spoke and did what was for others' good at His own expense. We must do the same.

We *will* pay when we confront the abuse we've been indulging. Risking others' anger and disapproval by describing how we've been sinned against will upset the status quo. It won't be easy being "real" with ourselves and others, but it will follow the example of Jesus.

On the other hand, we must also be willing to hear how we have damaged others by our own attitudes and behaviors. There must be mutuality of honesty about the impact of sin in the relationship.

2. Describe in a few sentences a recent event in which you were damaged by someone's words, attitude, or action.

3. Write what you might say to confront that person with the damage done to you, using "I" sentences ("I was hurt by your unkind words," or "I needed your support, not your anger, in that moment") rather than "you" sentences ("You are cruel," or "You never affirm me").

4. What response would you expect if you carried out the confrontation (i.e., how might you "pay" for your honesty)?

5. What words of confession might you need to say regarding your own damaging of the other person during that event?

Meet together to read this section and answer the questions. (30 minutes)

Repentance and Grace

The second ingredient of forgiveness is repentance. Jesus made it clear: "If your brother sins, rebuke him, and *if he repents*, forgive him" (Luke 17:3, emphasis added). Without repentance, there is no restoration of relationship. God requires it; so should we.

Repentance is not simply an apology but a turning of the heart back toward God and toward a commitment to the other's welfare. A superficial "I'm sorry" doesn't satisfy God. John the Baptizer warned, "Produce fruit in keeping with repentance" (Matthew 3:8). Words are cheap, and a shallow apology is easier than facing our sins of betrayal and rebellion. Yet God keeps calling us to open ourselves to the Spirit's convicting so that we can turn our hearts back toward Him and others time and time again.

However, repentance is not penance. Living out repentance through genuine behavior changes doesn't mean promising to "make it all up to you." We should desire and expect repentance without demanding penance.

Sometimes one person must wait a long time for another's repentance, standing ready to forgive before the other is ready to request or receive that forgiveness. When people can't admit damaging others, they can't repent, and full restoration of the relationship must be postponed. Often, though we long to offer forgiveness to our loved ones, we must first wait for them to acknowledge how they wounded us, enduring on their behalf the pain of a waiting love.

In the presence of honest confrontation and genuine repentance, grace is the third ingredient and the crowning glory of forgiveness. Grace cancels the debt owed and accepts the debtor without seeking revenge. God models it: When we turn from our sin, the Father offers us grace in Christ and welcomes us back into fellowship. Because God extends mercy to us, we extend it to others who don't deserve it, forgiving them in our hearts and then restoring them to relationship in the context of their continuing repentance and genuine change.

Forgiveness is both the hallmark and the foundation of genuine intimacy and mutual interdependence. Asking it requires an absence of defensiveness, and offering it demands an absence of revenge. Forgiveness must be reciprocal, specific, and continual; as long as we live this side of Home, we'll always need to seek and offer it to one another.

6. What do you think about the idea that you should become willing to forgive in your heart but should not restore relationship until the person repents?

7. Think of someone who has hurt you and has not repented. Do you think you are ready to forgive, or are you holding a grudge or looking for penance?

8. Name a recurring relational sin of yours that you are willing to acknowledge to the group; then discuss with the group what genuine repentance would look like for each sin. (For example, a woman who tries to control her husband might repent by not reminding him about a chore so he can decide on it himself; a man who is afraid to express his anger to his wife might write her a letter about how he feels.)

9. Discuss the practical problems that might develop if one partner in a relationship (a spouse, parent, child, etc.) refuses to repent (acknowledge and turn from sin) and the other person cannot restore him or her to full relationship.

Continue with your family group for the next section. (15 minutes)

Benefits of Mutual Interdependence

Learning to live in mutual interdependence with others is good for us. One of its greatest benefits is *spiritual vitality*. When learning to love imperfect human beings God's way, we must remain dependent on God and alive to our new spiritual identity in Him (including both our needs and our giftedness). Receiving grace from God and both offering and receiving it from others is the essence of our spirituality.

A second benefit of mutual interdependence is *a balanced view of self*. Recovering codependents must move from their old self-image (as martyr, rescuer, nobody, victim, etc.) into seeing and living out their new identity in Christ (as lover, encourager, confronter, grace-giver, etc.). We are no one's savior (not even our own), and that's good news because Jesus is all the Savior we need. But we are no one's slave or victim, either. We are new creatures with much to offer others because of the fountain of living water flowing from Jesus' life in us. We are not just repaired sinners with new power to fight temptation, but adopted children of the heavenly King with an entirely new identity for dealing with all of our relationships. That balanced view of self as precious but utterly God-dependent is a wonderful benefit as we live in mutual interdependence.

One final benefit is that mutual interdependence gives us a taste in this life of *genuine intimacy*—the bonding with others God designed us to enjoy. Genuine intimacy involves freedom, authenticity, acceptance, and forgiveness; all are made possible through our dependence on God, and all are experienced in freely chosen interdependence with others.

10. How does one imperfect person learning to live in mutual interdependence with another imperfect person keep us humbly dependent on God? Talk about your experience.

Prayer Requests

(10 minutes)
Share your prayer requests with other family members. Volunteer to pray specifically for one other person during the coming week.

My prayer request is _____

_____

and _____ is praying for me.

I am praying for _____ and his/her prayer request is _____

_____

_____.

LARGE GROUP

A Word of Hope
(10 minutes)

The words of the Apostle John are especially encouraging as we confront the sin in ourselves and others:

> **If we claim to be without sin, we deceive ourselves and the truth is not in us. If we confess our sins, he is faithful and just and will forgive us our sins and purify us from all unrighteousness. (1 John 1:8-9)**

Prayer

Those who wish may repeat the Lord's Prayer.

During the Week

Practice confronting in love this week when someone hurts you. Ask God to make you ready to forgive and to also admit your own sin in the situation. Record the events in your journal.

For more information on this week's topic, see *From Bondage to Bonding,* chapter 14. For more information regarding next week's topic, read chapter 15.

Benediction

Listen to the words of the Apostle Jude:

> **To him who is able to keep you from falling and to present you before his glorious presence without fault and with great joy—to the only God our Savior be glory, majesty, power and authority, through Jesus Christ our Lord, before all ages, now and forevermore! Amen. (Jude 24-25)**

Thinking God's Thoughts

Theme for meditation: GOD'S JUSTICE DEMANDS REPENTANCE.

Reading: 2 Chronicles 12:1-8
              Ezekiel 18:24-32
              Psalm 36:1-12
              Job 40:1-14, 42:6

Matthew 3:4-10
Galatians 6:1-8

Prayer:

Father, thank You for this evidence in Your Word that You are perfectly just:

Father, thank You for these areas in my life where Your justice calls me to repentance:

Father, this is what I will do (or stop doing) to live out my repentance:

FREE TO ABANDON DENIAL

LARGE GROUP

Perhaps these past months have been more difficult than you expected. Withdrawal from relationship addictions is often painful. Our codependency screams at us to resume our former way of life, but don't be discouraged. The process of recovery is worth pursuing.

Warm-up
(5 minutes)
1. Tell a person near you one concept about God that has changed for you in the past four or five months.

ON YOUR OWN

> Read this section to yourself and complete the exercises that follow.
> (20 minutes)

Embracing Who We Are

People who live in hot, muggy South Florida spend a lot of time in air-conditioned places with darkened windows. Emerging into daylight is always a shock, not just because of the heat and humidity, but also because of the blinding brightness. The adjustment can take a while.

Emerging from the darkness of *denial* into the glaring light of *reality* is a similar shock. The hidden, real self is unaccustomed to the light of openness and won't expect to be loved. In fact, we'll need God's grace to open ourselves both to self-discovery and to self-disclosure. We begin by finding and embracing who we really are.

First, we must admit we have *longings* for intimacy with our parents, our spouse, our children, our friends, and of course, God. In fact, we must actually embrace our longings, though it will feel like taking fire to our hearts. To be at peace with our legitimate yearnings for connectedness with God and others will take time, but it will restore us to our true humanness.

Second, we must acknowledge our *losses*. Where formerly we had numbed our anger and pain at life's disappointments, now we must enter the unfamiliar sunlight of honesty about how disappointing things were (or are) for us. We'll find we can survive in the daylight, and so can our love for our parents and for others who have harmed (or are harming) us. Grace frees us to no longer minimize, justify, or deny our losses, but to face them with integrity and grieve over them. We can be alive to every moment's reality, rejoicing over the gifts of grace offered us and mourning the pain of even the minor losses of each day.

Next, we must come out of denial regarding our *layers*—the ways we've hurt others by hiding our real selves behind protective masks. One of the most loving gifts we offer in relationships is authenticity. Yet we must admit we have not given others our hearts. We've continually looked back over our shoulders to wonder how we're doing or what others are thinking. We try to control things beyond our power to control, yet at the same time believe ourselves powerless when we should act boldly. In recovery we are called to face how our "false self" layers have kept us safe from pain but irresponsible about loving appropriately.

More than that, we must repent of our *antidependence* toward God, our dogged determination to make it in life without depending on Him. Our fists in God's face may be subtle, but God hasn't failed to get the message. Unless we acknowledge and repent of our determined spirit of antidependence, our hearts will harden to His call and our hands will be closed to His grace.

Step Four in the Twelve-Step program declares that in recovery "*we made a searching and fearless moral inventory of ourselves.*" For too long we shrank from taking inventory of our moral life because we wrongly believed our value lay in our ability to be perfect rather than in our preciousness. But in the context of God's mercy, honesty about our particular love failures opens us not to judgment but to grace. Our inventory will reveal us as worse than we thought we were—we don't do things right very often and then usually by accident. But the realization doesn't destroy us, because instead of rejection we find the unexpected steadiness of God's forgiveness. The discovery is sweet every time.

When we take a "moral inventory," we must also list our *giftedness*. It's easier to disbelieve we have something to offer than to use the gifts God has given us to bless others with who we are. The sunlight of reality will show us not just our love failures but our giftedness to fulfill our love obligations as well.

2. Complete the following sentences to do a mini-inventory of your inner self.

   a. One of my deepest longings regarding an important relationship is:

b. One of my most painful losses occurred in my relationship with

_____, when this happened:

c. I consider one of my greatest character weaknesses to be _____

_____;

this damages damages others by:

d. God is saddened when I do (or fail to do) this in relationship to Him:

e. One of God's best character gifts in me is _____,

with which I can bless others by:

Join together to read this section and discuss the questions. (30 minutes)

Abandoning Impression Management

Denial is the enemy of intimacy. When we do our "fourth-step work" of taking moral inventory, we open ourselves to genuine relationship with God if our hearts are moved to repentance and confession. When we stop denying our sin, our receiving of God's grace (available through the cross of Christ) reconnects us with God's mercy and fellowship.

We're also encouraged to confess our sins to others. Usually, when confronted with our weaknesses or love failures, we either pour contempt on ourselves, justify our behavior, or blame someone else for what went wrong. But James offers us an alternative: "Confess your sins to each other and pray for each other so that you may be healed" (James 5:16). God calls us not to pretend but to acknowledge our betrayal, not to blame but to grieve our inevitable wounding of one another.

The principle is expressed in AA's Step Five, which says that *we admitted to God, to ourselves, and to another human being the exact nature of our wrongs.* Generic confession won't do. We must talk honestly about exactly what we did to wrong (fail to love) people, including ourselves. Verbalizing our specific sins against God and others keeps us from slipping back into denial and keeps us moving forward into recovery.

The psalmist describes the painful consequences of our refusal to confess our sins:

When I kept silent,
my bones wasted away
through my groaning all day long.
For day and night
your hand was heavy upon me;
my strength was sapped
as in the heat of summer.
Then I acknowledged my sin to you

and did not cover up my iniquity.
I said, "I will confess
   my transgressions to the LORD"—
and you forgave
   the guilt of my sin. (Psalm 32:3-5)

Something important happens when we stop pretending we're better than we are and abandon our attempts at impression management (which sabotages intimacy in favor of self-protection). Confession is good for the soul and good for relationships as well. One of the best things about support groups like this one is the openness they encourage. We can drop our pretense and admit our honest struggles concerning life and faith, seeking help and finding not condemnation but acceptance and encouragement. If we the forgiven cannot offer openness and forgiveness—especially to fellow believers—we have missed our calling as ambassadors of Jesus' love.

3. How does your silence about your sin harm your relationship with God and others?

4. What good things happen when you confess your sin?

5. Share with your family group your answer to question 2c, regarding your greatest character weakness and how it damages others.

6. Now, one family group member should sit in the center of your circle while the other group members one at a time tell what they perceive to be one of God's best character gifts in that person and how it blesses others. Do this individually for each group member.

FAMILY GROUP

| Remain together for this section. |
| (15 minutes) |

Receiving Grace

It's not enough just to admit our wrongs to ourselves, God, and others. The purpose of our moral inventory is not self-contempt (hating ourselves) or self-improvement (perfecting ourselves), but genuine repentance and the receiving of grace. Grace woos us from sin and makes us willing to live out our sorrow for sin by turning from it.

The first phase of repentance that is really lived out in our lives is expressed in AA's Step Six, which says that *"we were entirely ready to have God remove all these defects of character"* exposed in our moral inventory. It won't be easy. Our inner pull toward self-sufficiency and lovelessness is reinforced by years of bad habits and an inclination toward rebellion and unbelief. We love our sin and don't want to give it up.

If we wait until we hate our sin, however, we may never let it go. If we're *willing* to hate it more and more (because we see how it harms God, ourselves, and others), then God's Spirit will wean us from our character defects and salt our thirst for His grace. When we're ready to release our wrong designs for living, God will give us grace to live without them.

Coming out of denial must eventually bring us to the final step in repentance: turning from our sin. Step Seven declares that we approached God and *"humbly asked him to remove our shortcomings."* What is lacking in this step—and it is a significant omission from a biblical perspective—is the basis on which we can ask God for anything, particularly the removal of our shortcomings (sins). According to the Bible, sin-removal is made possible by receiving Jesus' blood sacrifice as payment for our sins. In fact, Christ's atonement is the *only* basis on which we can ask God to remove our shortcomings and escape our codependency.

God removes our shortcomings in two senses. First, He removes our sin legally, granting us forgiveness for our sins because of our faith in Jesus' satisfaction of the death penalty we deserve for our sin. God also removes sin from our daily living, helping us through His Spirit to stop doing what we shouldn't do and increasingly do what we ought to do—not so that He will love us but because He already does.

7. Many people find it hard to accept that Jesus had to die in order for God to forgive them. "Why can't God just forgive without a human sacrifice?" they ask. The question is worth taking seriously. Which of the following statements do you accept? Which do you not accept, and why?

- Rebellion against our Creator is a capital offense. Traitors against a King deserve the death penalty.

- Justice is an essential part of God's character. Actions must have consequences. When humans spurn God, abuse each other, and mar their world, someone must bear the consequences.

- Love is an essential part of God's character. He knows that the just consequence of our actions is death, yet He desires to save our lives so that we can live as His friends. He is willing to bear the consequence Himself.

- Jesus is God, who took on our humanness and bore the just consequences of our rebellion when He died on the cross in our place. Our debts and crimes didn't evaporate when we apologized; God paid for them Himself.

8. How do you feel after reading these statements? Does all of this seem abstract? Do you find it hard or easy to get excited about it?

9. If there is time, compose with your group a prayer of praise to God for Jesus' blood shed for you.

Prayer Requests

(10 minutes)

Share your prayer requests with other family members. Volunteer to pray specifically for one other person during the coming week.

My prayer request is _____

_____

and _____ is praying for me.

I am praying for _____ and his/her prayer request is _____

_____

_____ .

A Word of Hope

(10 minutes)

These words of Isaiah remind us that we won't be totally free of sin until we're Home. Yet even in our sin,

> **The LORD longs to be gracious to [us];**
> **he rises to show [us] compassion. (Isaiah 30:18)**

Prayer

Those who wish may repeat the Lord's Prayer.

During the Week

Pray that God will lead you to a spiritual "guide"—a mature believer who will listen to your "moral inventory" without criticizing, acknowledge your weaknesses without trying to change you, and affirm your strengths without pushing you. Ask that person sometime this week to become your mentor, and set up a regular time to talk together over the coming months. If your "first choice" is unavailable or proves unacceptable, pray for an alternate until you find the right person.

Also, read the Apostle Paul's chapter on mutual love, 1 Corinthians 13. Consider memorizing it, beginning one verse at a time.

For more information on this week's topic, see *From Bondage to Bonding,* chapter 15. For more information regarding next week's topic, read chapter 16.

Benediction

Receive in your hearts these words from the writer of the book of Hebrews:

> **May the God of peace, who through the blood of the eternal covenant brought back from the dead our Lord Jesus, that great Shepherd of the sheep, equip you with everything good for doing his will, and may he work in us what is pleasing to him, through Jesus Christ, to whom be glory for ever and ever. Amen. (Hebrews 13:20)**

Thinking God's Thoughts

Theme for meditation: GOD REVEALS HIMSELF.

Reading:
       Exodus 6:1-8
       Isaiah 40:1-3
       Psalm 25:4, Proverbs 29:18
       Romans 1:18-25
       John 17:1-8
       Ephesians 1:15-23

Prayer:
       Father, thank You for this evidence in Your Word that You make Yourself known:
       Father, thank You for these areas in my life where You've shown Yourself to me:
       Father, this is what I will do both to know You and to make myself known to You:

FREE TO LET GO OF CONTROL

Welcome! We're in the process of examining what mutual interdependence looks like, and mutual freedom is this session's topic—one of the most essential ingredients of intimate relationship. Much as two people might want each other to change, both must be willing to stop demanding that change happen. The freedom that moves us toward intimacy is not merely freedom *from* but freedom *to*—freedom from our codependent compulsion with all its fear and loneliness, and freedom to love without control or manipulation.

Warm-up
(5 minutes)

1. Tell somebody one good thing that happened in your relationship with God during the past week.

> Read this section to yourself, then answer the questions.
> (15 minutes)

Releasing Demandingness

Because freedom is essential to intimacy, we must ask how it is possible to abandon our control strategies and free one another from our mutual demandingness. To begin with, we must recognize that communion with God is what makes freedom possible. God frees us to be who we are by loving us just as we are, and we are changed by His grace. He thus models how we are to offer grace.

At the same time He also enables us (through His Spirit) to offer grace to others, giving us resources beyond ourselves for loving them even at their worst. When we ask God to give us His own love for them, an amazing grace enters our hearts and provides us with a compassion utterly beyond our own limited capacity. There may be no rush of affection, but we can choose to act on behalf of other people's good, offering them God's confrontation and His grace without hypocrisy. We connect ourselves to God's work in this world when we do what Jesus came to do: offer others freedom by confronting and accepting them just as they are in Jesus' name, with the intention of inviting them into repentance and grace.

Freedom is perhaps the most precious gift we offer another human being. Like charity, it must begin at home, as we offer ourselves the freedom to be ourselves. Because of God's acceptance we can let go of impression management and start just *living*. We can stop obligating and being obligated in our relationships. We can live unpretentiously because we know we are precious to God, and no one else's rejection has power to destroy us. We can gift ourselves with freedom.

Then we can gift others with a similar freedom—to be who they are without trying to make them change. We will long for them to become more Christlike and we'll confront them when they're not, but we won't take responsibility for making it happen.

Letting go of our demandingness can be a lengthy and painful process. We must practice abandoning our control strategies one at a time, asking God to release us from our compulsion to manage other people's lives. Finally He will free us to no longer *have* to have others "behave" in order to be at peace within ourselves.

2. Name one of the most important people in your life and tell what you most want to change or control in that person.

3. What do you generally do to try to change or control that person?

4. What positive consequences might occur if you stopped demanding or controlling?

5. What negative consequences might occur if you stopped demanding or controlling?

6. Picture yourself hanging over a cliff, clutching for dear life to an outcropping bush. Imagine God saying, "Let go and I'll catch you." How do you feel about the idea that God wants you to let go of the bush (your self-protective strategies) with no guarantee of how long you'll have to face the sickening sense of falling before He catches you? What will you do if He takes His time about making you feel secure?

Briefly discuss what you discovered about yourself in questions 2 through 6. Then read the next section and complete the exercises.
(25 minutes)

FAMILY GROUP

Facing and Dealing with Our Imperfection

Nobody's perfect, but codependents think they should always be trying harder. God is a Holy God who calls us to holy living, but that doesn't mean we're perfectible in this life. In fact, the purpose of grace is not to make us perfect, but to show us our need for a Savior, then show us the Savior we need, then create in us a burning desire to be more like Him. In this life our fallenness is interwoven with our humanness, and we'll be imperfect until we're Home. We don't always have to be right or even understood; we can let others find us imperfect. And we can offer others freedom to be imperfect, too. It will cause us pain when someone disappoints us, but we won't die and we don't have to leave the relationship because of it.

Freedom to be imperfect doesn't excuse us from dealing with our imperfections, however. We ought never become glad about our imperfection; God gives us a holy dissatisfaction with our sin. When we wrong others, we must repent and change. We begin by owning the sins of our past. AA's Step Eight says that *"we made a list of all persons we had harmed, and became willing to make amends to them all."* Our list must be specific, naming both the persons and our sin against those persons. We must unflinchingly accept our guilt for the damage done through our irresponsibility or malice and become willing to admit our wrongs without self-justification.

It will be risky approaching people we've treated badly, asking their forgiveness and seeking their good. AA's Step Nine says that *"we made direct amends to [people we had harmed] wherever possible, except when to do so would injure them or others."* There is a fundamental danger in the concept of "making amends," as though we could somehow atone for our wrongs through something we might do or say. Grace, not compensation, must be the foundation of our restoration process. Making amends is not penance but repentance—asking forgiveness with an acknowledgment of our wrong and a commitment to change. The keys to risking wisely are our desire for restoration in the relationship and our commitment to the good of everyone involved. Clearing our own conscience is less the goal than blessing the other person with our repentance. When "making amends" merely reopens old wounds or is abusive to anyone, it is best to simply repent before God.

7. Take five minutes to individually make a list of persons you've harmed; be as specific as possible.

FAMILY GROUP

8. What might be the best way to confess and/or make amends to the person(s) you harmed?

Discuss question 8, and then do the following section together.
(25 minutes)

Mutual Freedom

What does it mean to offer ourselves and others mutual freedom? Consider this partial list of what we can become free to do or to be.

First, we're free to have feelings—though actually, we cannot help but have feelings. Our emotional responses to the events of our lives come naturally, yet for many codependents certain emotions are difficult to acknowledge because they were "forbidden" in childhood. In the face of those childhood rules of silence, we must occasionally remind ourselves that feelings are okay. In fact, once we own and feel them, they no longer have the power to control or destroy us, especially with the Holy Spirit helping us choose whether to express them to anyone besides God, to act on them or not, and so on. We must free others to have their own feelings, too, even when those emotions make us uncomfortable or afraid. We must no longer judge others for their feelings, though we might insist they express them nondestructively.

Second, we're free to have needs—emotional, physical, and spiritual. We may feel that everyone's needs but our own are valid—that's not true. It's appropriate to ask others (a family member, counselor, doctor, or friend) to meet our needs. We can request a teenager to play the radio someplace else or not at all, ask a spouse or friend for a hug, or make an appointment to talk with a counselor. It will feel demanding— having needs at all feels demanding to a codependent. But when we deny our neediness, we intensify our self-sufficiency toward God and shut ourselves off from mutual interdependence with people. We also must let others have needs and not feel guilty if we can't meet them all. We don't have to solve everyone's problems.

Third, we're free to make responsible choices: We acknowledge that there are some things we can't change or control, while other things are definitely our responsibility and no one else's. Usually we confuse the two. Simply stated, we ought to take responsibility for our own growth, attitudes, and behavior, and then give God control over everything else. We can't control our feelings, but we can own them as ours and we can choose how to act, asking God's Spirit to show us what we must do and when. On the other hand, we must offer others freedom over their own actions, too. We can stop being caretakers and let others do what they can do for themselves. We can stop rescuing others, refusing to interfere with the natural consequences of their choices. It will feel unloving, even cruel, to hold others accountable for their own lives and emotions, but it is deeply respectful of their personhood and is therefore truly loving.

This appropriate "division of responsibility" (each person responsible only for himself) is an ongoing process that keeps short accounts with God, self, and others. AA's Step Ten declares that *"we continued to take personal inventory, and when we were wrong promptly admitted it."* Humility and willingness to repent and ask forgiveness must become a way of life, not just a once-and-for-all event.

9. What feelings were you *not* allowed to have or express as a child? As an adult? Tell the group how you might have or express those feelings now.

10. Tell why or in what ways it was (is) dangerous or shameful for you to have needs as a child or as an adult. Tell the group how you might express your needs now.

11.   a. What is one action (your own) you will take responsibility for this week?

b. What is one action (someone else's) you will refuse to take responsibility for this week? Think of something you habitually try to control.

Prayer Requests
(10 minutes)
Share your prayer requests with other family members. Volunteer to pray specifically for one other person during the coming week.

My prayer request is _____

_____

and _____ is praying for me.

I am praying for _____ and his/her prayer request is _____

_____

_____.

A Word of Hope
(10 minutes)
The Apostle Paul encourages us to keep going in our process of biblical recovery, telling the Philippian believers (and us):

This is my prayer: that your love may abound more and more in knowledge and depth of insight, so that you may be able to discern what is best and may be pure and blameless until the day of Christ, filled with the fruit of righteousness that comes through Jesus Christ—to the glory and praise of God. (Philippians 1:9-11)

Prayer
All who wish may join in repeating the Serenity Prayer.

During the Week
Share with your mentor the list you made of persons you had harmed, and discuss what (if anything) you can do to make amends.

Also, another freedom we can enjoy is the freedom to be spontaneous—to enter the unknown without self-protection. Spontaneity can't be programmed or controlled; as soon as we try to make it happen, we keep it from happening. But we can practice and offer the freedom to just have fun. Deliberately plan one fun event with another recovering codependent this week. (You may have to take a noncodependent along to show you how to play.)

For more information on this week's topic, see *From Bondage to Bonding,* chapter 16. For more information regarding next week's topic, read chapter 17.

Benediction

Hear the words of God through the Apostle Peter:

Grow in the grace and knowledge of our Lord and Savior Jesus Christ. To him be glory both now and forever! Amen. (2 Peter 3:18)

Thinking God's Thoughts

Theme for meditation: GOD ACCEPTS OUR DEVOTED HEARTS.

Reading: Genesis 6:1-9
            2 Samuel 24:10-25
            Psalm 119:105-112
            Job 42:7-9
            Acts 10:23-35
            Romans 15:1-7

Prayer:
    Father, thank You for this evidence in Your Word that You accept a heart turned toward You:
    Father, thank You for this evidence in my life that You accept my heart's devotion:
    Father, this is what I will do (or stop doing) to express my heart's commitment to love You and others:

SPIRITUAL VITALITY

LARGE GROUP

"One-three-eleven" summarizes the spiritual focus of AA's Twelve-Step recovery program. Step One exposes our helplessness to manage our lives without God; Step Three stresses God's care as we turn our lives and wills over to Him; and Step Eleven deals with our ongoing connectedness and obedience to God. During this session we will explore Step Eleven.

Warm-up
(5 minutes)
1. Tell someone what fun thing you did (or at least what you set specific plans to do) this past week.

ON YOUR OWN

> Read this section to yourself and answer the questions that follow.
> (20 minutes)

Connected to God
Step Eleven of AA's Twelve-Step program declares that *"we sought through prayer and meditation to improve our conscious contact with God as we understood him, praying only for knowledge of his will for us and the power to carry that out."* That commitment to pursue God-connectedness flows from our realization that His love is what we were designed to most deeply want and enjoy. God's heart leans toward those whose hearts yearn for and seek after Him. If we hunger after God for our very life, we are never disappointed.

However, a determined pursuit after God through prayer and meditation is often distasteful to us, not just because we're too busy to be quiet, but because prayer and meditation say something about us we hate to admit. Prayer (humble worship and communication with God) says we're dependent creatures who have to ask for what we cannot provide for ourselves. It reminds us of our inability to control our own lives and puts to death our insistence on "doing it my way." Meditation (taking time to enjoy God and to think His thoughts as they apply to our lives) forces us to wait for God's direction instead of acting impulsively out of self-interest.

Of course, prayer and meditation don't automatically usher us into God's presence nor communicate His grace to us. Grace doesn't respond to formulas, especially if our prayers are rote or our meditation is merely intellectual. Nevertheless, unless we quiet our spirits in a posture of asking, receiving, worshiping, and enjoying, we can't sustain the relationship with God that brings us Life.

Our commitment to improve our conscious contact with God is the cornerstone of our recovery process. Bonding with God is our most important work, giving meaning to our lives and enabling us to love Him and others with boldness and passion. We cannot give what we have not received, so we desperately need God's gift of bonding. Just as an infant needs the parents to bond with him or her quite apart from anything the infant has done or can do for them, so we need God to bond with us simply because He loves us. We can't give love away unless we've first received it from God.

God connects with us, His children, by offering us His love and by allowing us to impact Him. His love was most clearly demonstrated when He "sent his Son as an atoning sacrifice for our sins" (1 John 4:10). God bonded with us at the cost of His Son's death on our behalf. There's never been a love to equal that.

God also allows us to have impact on Him. What we do or feel *matters* to Him. Our sin wounds the heart of God, and He grieves over the wrongs of His beloved children (Ephesians 4:30). Jesus also taught that "there is rejoicing in the presence of the angels of God over one sinner who repents" (Luke 15:10). Our relational choices call forth God's involved response, and our confusion and weakness call forth His fervent intercession on our behalf: "The Spirit helps us in our weakness. We do not know what we ought to pray for, but the Spirit himself intercedes for us with groans that words cannot express" (Romans 8:26). How amazing that the God of the universe cares for us with such a steady and impassioned love.

2. What signs do you see in your life that you are . . .

  • getting closer to God?

• still pretty far from God?

3. Think back on an incident from this past week that occurred in relationship with someone you know well. As God was present during that incident and saw inside your heart, do you think He was glad or sorrowful? Describe what you imagine the look on His face was as He reacted to your words, attitude, and behavior in that incident.

4. Make a list of the things that keep you from the kind of prayer or meditation that would strengthen your heart-connection to God—not just the external things (busy-ness, fatigue, etc.) but internal factors as well (pride, anger, fear, arrogance, etc.).

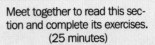

Meet together to read this section and complete its exercises.
(25 minutes)

FAMILY GROUP

Free to Trust

AA's Step Eleven also declares that in our recovery process we must pray to know and obey God's will for our lives. What *is* God's will for our lives? "Man's chief end," according to the Westminster Shorter Catechism, "is to glorify God, and to enjoy him forever."[1] Doing God's will involves honoring and worshiping Him, not just in church but in every phase of living. Worship means acknowledging God as God and quieting our spirits in reverence before Him. Contrary to rebellious autonomy, the worshiping heart accepts itself as under God's care and authority, particularly in those circumstances we'd most like to change—even when we don't understand it, don't like it, and wouldn't have chosen it. We may not literally bend our knees every time we worship, but we can bend our hearts before God anytime and anywhere we find a quiet moment in His presence. It is His will that we worship Him.

God also calls us to believe (trust) in Him. Jesus said, "The work of God is this: to believe in the one he has sent" (John 6:29). If what God desires is faith in His Son, Jesus, then we as codependents must rethink our former lifestyle. We've always been doers, accomplishers, goal-directed achievers; we've even tried hard to be spiritual. It's a shock to learn that the opposite of sin is not virtue but faith, not doing good but trusting in Jesus' sacrifice on our behalf.

Jesus calls us to live out our faith by finding our rest in Him. How unlike the hurried, often frenzied pace we codependents are accustomed to! We'd much rather be in charge, self-sufficient, controlling. Resting doesn't come easily to recovering codependents. We'd rather give than receive, wear ourselves out than ask for help. It is to us that Jesus' words seem most directed:

"Come to me, all you who are weary and burdened, and I will give you rest. Take my yoke upon you and learn from me, for I am gentle and humble in heart, and you will find rest for your souls. For my yoke is easy and my burden is light." (Matthew 11:28-30)

5. When and where do you find worship most meaningful? Why?

6. In what ways have you enjoyed God during the last several months?

7. As a group write a psalm or prayer to God, including one or two sentences for each of the following. When you finish, repeat the psalm or prayer together.

• Praise and worship for who He is

• Confession regarding how and why you avoid worship

- Confession regarding how and why you don't trust Him

- Acknowledgment of your need and desire for Him

- Gratitude for His faithful love

FAMILY GROUP

Remain together for the next section.
(20 minutes)

Free to Obey

Though none of us escapes the rebellion and self-centeredness resulting from the Fall, loved children generally seek to please and be pleasing to their parents. Likewise, our redeemed nature as beloved children of God draws us toward obedience. When we know we belong to Someone who loves us, we want to please the One to whom we belong. According to AA's Step Eleven, in recovery *"we pray for knowledge of [God's] will for us and the power to carry that out."* Our obedience to God's will is not a way to earn (or keep) God's love but an overflow of His love in us and through us toward others. "If you love me," Jesus said, "you will obey what I command" (John 14:15).

The only encouragement we have that we are able to love as Jesus loved is that He has given us His Spirit to do in us what we cannot do in our own strength. Step Eleven specifically mentions praying for "the power to carry . . . out" God's will for us, and that power is available to believers through the Holy Spirit.

It is not a power we strive to obtain; we simply use what is already there. Jesus compared it to a branch bearing fruit simply because it remains attached to a vine (John 15:1-8). Branches don't strain to produce grapes; grapes just *happen* because the branches they're growing on are connected to the source of nourishment. We can't generate the power to obey God's will. The power comes from staying in fellowship with God.

If we obey, we'll suffer. It won't be comfortable or convenient or popular for us to stop acting as codependents. But if we abide in Jesus and act like He acted, we'll find He will be there to sustain us in the aftermath of our right choices. We can exchange self-effort for surrender, self-protection for risky love, self-preoccupation for other-centeredness. As we allow the Holy Spirit of Jesus to direct our choices through Scripture reading, time with mature believers, and time in prayer, we'll have all the power we need to do what He says.

8. Consider what Jesus said was the greatest of God's commands: "Love the Lord your God with all your heart and with all your soul and with all your mind. This is the first and greatest commandment. And the second is like it: Love your neighbor as yourself" (Matthew 22:37-40). Martin Luther said it this way: "Love God and do what you please." Discuss whether or not (and why) it would be biblical to live according to Luther's prescription.

9. Loving God and trusting Him go together. Discuss some specific ways you might show this week that you trust God in your most important relationships. (Trusting God would also involve doing truly loving things for others—what is for their good—without protecting yourself from the consequences.)

Prayer Requests

(10 minutes)
Share your prayer requests with other family members. Volunteer to pray specifically for one other person during the coming week.

My prayer request is _____

_____

and _____ is praying for me.

I am praying for _____ and his/her prayer request is _____

_____

_____.

A Word of Hope

(10 minutes)
As you pursue connectedness with God this week, remember the promise given those who have faith in Him:

Anyone who comes to him [God] must believe that he exists and that he rewards those who earnestly seek him. (Hebrews 11:6)

Prayer

All who wish may join in repeating the Serenity Prayer.

During the Week

Choose one or more of these psalms to use in private worship this week: Psalm 23, 25, 27, 32, 34, or a psalm of your own choosing. Read the psalm aloud to God, personalizing the ideas, using "I" or your own name, and addressing God as though He were sitting across from you. (Example from Psalm 23: Lord, You are my good shepherd and I am Your sheep, Your responsibility. I shall not be in want—I have all I need to sustain me physically, emotionally, and spiritually because of Your reliable and loving provision for me.)

For more information on this week's topic, see *From Bondage to Bonding,* chapter 17. For more information regarding next week's topic, read chapter 18.

Benediction

Hear the ancient priestly blessing:

> **The LORD bless you**
> **and keep you;**
> **the LORD make his face shine upon you**
> **and be gracious to you;**
> **the LORD turn his face toward you**
> **and give you peace. (Numbers 6:24-26)**

Thinking God's Thoughts

Theme for meditation: GOD REWARDS CHOSEN OBEDIENCE.

Reading:
        Exodus 20:1-17
        Jeremiah 17:5-10
        Psalm 19:7-14
        Proverbs 11:18, 19:17
        Matthew 5:7-12
        Revelation 22:12-17

Prayer:
    Father, thank You for this evidence in Your Word that You reward Your
        obedient children:
    Father, thank You for the ways You have blessed my life when I've obeyed You:
    Father, this is what I will do (or stop doing) to trust You with my life and to
        obey Your command to love:

NOTE

1. *The Westminster Standards* (Philadelphia, PA: Great Commission Publications), page 71.

SACRIFICIAL LOVE

Congratulations! This session marks the final step in a courageous and perhaps difficult journey over the past six months. Though this will be the last structured meeting of this healing community, you may wish to maintain a relationship of some kind with either this group or one like it. You may not need as much intensive work as you've been doing during recent months, but your journey into healthy relationships will last your entire lifetime, and Christian friends will always be an important part of that journey. Also, you may now be in a position to help others begin or continue a similar journey. May our good heavenly Father guide you in your ongoing process toward Home.

Warm-up
(5 minutes)
 1. Tell someone one thing about this group experience that has helped you the most during the last six months.

> Complete this section individually.
> (20 minutes)

Bonding with Others
God has called us to move out of the bondage of codependency and into genuine bonding. Bonding is the love-connection we enjoy with God and others that motivates us to worship and trust God and to do for others whatever is for their ultimate well-being. Love must characterize who we are and will determine what we do.

　　Bonding with God and knowing we belong to Him is the basis for healing all losses and rebuilding all broken relationships. The intent of God's grace is always restoration to community, and the stronger our bond with Him, the greater our capacity for mutual interdependence with others. AA's twelfth step affirms this double commitment to God and others: *"Having had a spiritual awakening as the result of these Steps, we tried to carry this message to others, and to practice these principles in all our affairs."* Our new spiritual vitality makes us long to bless others with the hope we've discovered, and our focus shifts from self-preoccupation to other-centeredness.

There are different levels of bonding as we move into mutual interdependence with the people who occupy our lives. We may wish, for example, to strengthen our bondedness with our *parents.* To the degree the parental bond was inadequate or lost in childhood we must acknowledge to ourselves the anger and grief that accompanied its loss. Loving our parents God's way may also mean confronting them with the nurturing losses we suffered because of their addiction or abuse. Such confrontation should reveal their failure to have met our needs, but it ought not destroy them in the process. Our intention should be to invite them to ongoing repentance that will open them to God's grace and our forgiveness. This kind of bold love will terrify us, and it may not "pay off" in a more intimate relationship with our parents, especially at first. But if we are to live out our own repentance, we must ask God to show us how to offer a right kind of love to our parents.

We also long to strengthen our bondedness with our *spouse, adult children,* and *close friends.* Intimate relationships are always a matter of the heart. When addiction is present, commitments of the heart are compromised and the addiction must be addressed before genuine bonding can become reality. The process of honesty and personal change may take some time, and offering one's whole heart may need to be postponed until the other is ready to receive it. The one we love deeply may be unable to hear the depth of our pain or to share the burden of our self-discoveries. We may need to suffer the loneliness of a waiting love, walking the tightrope of inviting the other in without revictimizing ourselves. In some cases, we may need to relinquish the dream of deep intimacy with that person and turn to God with our overflowing hearts. In His own time and way, God may heal the relationship if both will be honest, repent their lack of love, lean hard on God, and change wrong habits, one day at a time.

The connecting we do with our *casual friends* is different in degree from that which we pursue with our spouse, parents, adult children, or closest companions. There are those who can receive only some of what we have to offer. Jesus touched hundreds of lives through His teaching and healing, but He opened His heart to only a few. Yet in all of His interactions with both friends and antagonists, Jesus offered His true self. He didn't pretend; He didn't put on airs; He didn't try to protect Himself. He just was who He was. And we can do the same—just be ourselves, offering our acceptance and compassion out of the overflow of God's acceptance and compassion toward us.

2. Across the top of the next two pages, write the names of two or three adults with whom you most wish to bond in mutual interdependence. Put a check next to the names of those who share your desire for mutual bonding at this time.

Then, for each name do the following:

• List the primary obstacle(s) to mutual interdependence (from both sides).

• Write what you think God wants you to do in terms of loving confrontation and/or forgiveness.

• Write a prayer for restoration with that person based on mutual repentance and change.

NAMES

OBSTACLES

ACTIONS

PRAYER

NAMES

OBSTACLES

ACTIONS

PRAYER

FAMILY GROUP

Join with your family group for this section.
(25 minutes)

Chosen Suffering

Bonding is the goal and fruit of our healing process, but it can't develop without substantial risks of faith. Jesus commissioned His disciples to "love each other as I have loved you. Greater love has no one than this, that he lay down his life for his friends" (John 15:12-13). We're to love others by giving up our lives for them.

When we abandon our codependency, we abandon life as we've known it, and it will feel like death. Not being in charge, letting others be who they are, refusing to run from conflict, facing our own and others' anger, living by grace instead of achievement—what brings us into life always feels like death. And that's what God wills us to choose: death to our comfortable self-centeredness and entry into the terror of grace. Our illusions must die, and so must our demandingness that God and others "be there" for us. In exchange for our codependency God offers us (along with His presence) perplexity, pain, loneliness, and a lingering sorrow only Home will assuage. In choosing life we must first choose death. That's what it means to love.

If there's one thing codependents are good at, it's suffering. We pity ourselves and complain that we have no choice, but inwardly we pride ourselves in it. Suffering is a compulsion; we unconsciously seek out situations where we must give more than we receive, and we feel cheated if there's no pain for us to endure. However, the suffering involved in appropriate bonding is another thing altogether. It is not victimization but a willingness to act in another person's best interest even if we must suffer for it. The difference lies in its purpose.

Chosen suffering is not self-directed—trying to win approval, admiration, or sympathy for oneself by being in pain. Rather, it is other-directed—enduring patiently the pain that may come as the result of doing whatever is necessary to offer strong love. Instead of being in bondage to the whims of others for our own sakes, we are free to choose to suffer for the sake of others. Jesus *chose* to leave Heaven and face the Cross for His beloved. Knowing Himself to be God but "not [considering] equality with God something to be grasped" (Philippians 2:6), He took "the very nature of a servant" (verse 7)—operating from a position of inner, personal strength in His sacrificial love.

Christlike setting aside of our own comfort or convenience for the sake of doing constructive good for others is a powerful and productive kind of suffering. Its purpose is to draw others to Christ, not to draw attention to ourselves. We face the pain of standing ever ready to offer our hearts, not so we'll be loved, but because it is our redeemed nature to love selflessly as Jesus loved. His Spirit generates other-centeredness in us and keeps us doggedly committed to sacrificial living. Instead of giving up when our suffering doesn't get the results we expect, we can look again at God's patient longsuffering toward our own slowness of heart and then lean into others' resistance with continued love by His strength. To the degree Christ is given a free hand to live through us, we will love sacrificially. It is our *new* nature.

3. Give a specific example from your own life of self-centered suffering (suffering that keeps you safe or "in charge" emotionally).

4. Tell one thing you might choose to do for someone you love that would cost you suffering (waiting, confronting in love, refusing to rescue, etc.).

5. What codependent strategies have you begun to put to death over the past six months? (Be specific.)

6. Which of your codependent strategies must yet be put to death so that you can offer greater authenticity and freedom in your relationships? Are there any you are ready to give up now?

FAMILY GROUP

Remain together to read the next section and complete the exercises.
(20 minutes)

Paradoxes of Grace Living: A Process

Our Christlike chosen suffering is not just the result of others' failure to meet our need for love and involvement. Even when bonding with others offers us wonderful tastes of intimacy, we suffer because we're alive to our insatiable longing for more—more than anyone can give in this life. In many ways we'll be more lonely than ever, just because we've tasted sweet intimacy with God and others. Those luminous moments with God and the ones we love happen when we least expect or deserve them, and they leave us bereft when they pass. Once we've experienced grace living, nothing else satisfies. Grace blesses with its fierceness and makes us desperate for more, but we cannot extend our grace experiences or save them for a rainy day; they don't stay and are never enough and can't be reproduced at will.

Yet recovery is ambiguous and relapses are inevitable. Though our experiences of divine and human grace seduce us relentlessly, we also fear genuine freedom with all its responsibilities for grace-based, love-dominated living. It feels more normal to be persecuted, hating those who keep us in bondage. Loneliness, helplessness, loss of attachments—all our worst fears are realized in the wilderness of our recovery journey. In the desert our fists go up and we call God cruel for delivering us from codependency. "Thanks, but no thanks," we snarl at Him.

Then He comes to us again in His shining brightness and His compassion, offering us grace for our recovery relapse. It's never a question of whether or not God still loves us. His grace always flows in our direction, uninterrupted, sweet, ready to embrace who we deeply are as soon as we turn back toward Him. It is we who interrupt the flow, who choose our addictions over His grace, who act on fear, not faith, who deaden our souls by medicating our pain instead of walking through the pain, our hand in His. We hold the power to choose life or death, and the more we choose life, the more our addictions show themselves for what they really are—death-bound strategies that can never deliver the delight they promise.

Our culture will consider us weird, but the Apostle John assures us with these words:

> **How great is the love the Father has lavished on us, that we should be called children of God! And that is what we are! The reason the world does not know us is that it did not know him. Dear friends, now we are children of God, and what we will be has not yet been made known. But we know that when he appears, we shall be like him for we shall see him as he is. (1 John 3:1-2)**

For the hope set before us, we can endure the shame of our restoration process.

Until Home, as we wander (sometimes aimlessly, it seems) through the desert of our recovery, God has promised to grace us with the joy of His forgiveness, wonderful tastes of freedom through His Life in us, and the comfort of His Presence in every sorrow. He calls us to offer that same grace to others as well, then gives us the power to do so. The journey from bondage to bonding is a journey into our Father's endless embrace.

7. Tell about one time during the past months when you've enjoyed a special taste of God's gracious love for you.

8. God always calls us to restoration of community, especially within our families. Tell how God is turning your heart back to your parents, brothers, sisters, spouse, and/or children in your healing process.

FAMILY GROUP

Prayer Requests

(10 minutes)

Share your prayer requests with other family members. Volunteer to pray specifically for one other person during the coming week.

My prayer request is _____

_____

and _____ is praying for me.

I am praying for _____ and his/her prayer request is _____

LARGE GROUP

A Word of Hope

(10 minutes)

The Apostle Paul encourages us as believers with these words:

> **I thank my God every time I remember you. In all my prayers for all of you, I always pray with joy because of your partnership in the gospel from the first day until now, being confident of this, that he who began a good work in you will carry it on to completion until the day of Christ Jesus. (Philippians 1:3-6)**

Prayer

Those who wish may repeat the Lord's Prayer.

During the Week

Pray about whether or not (and with whom) God might have you continue to meet regularly for mutual encouragement and accountability in your ongoing healing process from bondage to bonding. For more information on this week's topic, see *From Bondage to Bonding,* chapter 18.

Benediction

Receive these words of comfort from the Apostle Peter:

> **The God of all grace, who called you to his eternal glory in Christ, after you have suffered a little while, will himself restore you and make you strong, firm and steadfast. To him be the power for ever and ever. Amen. . . . Peace to all of you who are in Christ. (1 Peter 5:10-11,14)**

Thinking God's Thoughts

Theme for meditation: GOD RESTORES THOSE WHO SUFFER.

Reading:　　　Isaiah 61:1-7
　　　　　　　Joel 2:12-27
　　　　　　　Psalm 22:1-31
　　　　　　　Job 42:10-17
　　　　　　　Luke 16:19-31
　　　　　　　Hebrews 12:1-13

Prayer:
　　　Father, thank You for this evidence in Your Word that You care about those who suffer:
　　　Father, thank You for this evidence in my life that You care about my suffering:
　　　Father, this is what I will do (or stop doing) to share Your life by choosing to suffer for others' good: